# Counseling
# the Sick
# and Terminally Ill

RESOURCES FOR
CHRISTIAN COUNSELING

# RESOURCES FOR CHRISTIAN COUNSELING

1. Innovative Approaches to Counseling   *Gary R. Collins*
2. Counseling Christian Workers   *Louis McBurney*
3. Self-Talk, Imagery, and Prayer in Counseling
   *H. Norman Wright*
4. Counseling Those with Eating Disorders
   *Raymond E. Vath*
5. Counseling the Depressed   *Archibald D. Hart*
6. Counseling for Family Violence and Abuse
   *Grant L. Martin*
7. Counseling in Times of Crisis
   *Judson J. Swihart and Gerald C. Richardson*
8. Counseling and Guilt   *Earl D. Wilson*
9. Counseling and the Search for Meaning   *Paul R. Welter*
10. Counseling for Unplanned Pregnancy and Infertility
    *Everett L. Worthington, Jr.*
11. Counseling for Problems of Self-Control
    *Richard P. Walters*
12. Counseling for Substance Abuse and Addiction
    *Stephen Van Cleave, Walter Byrd, Kathy Revell*
13. Counseling and Self-Esteem   *David E. Carlson*
14. Counseling Families   *George A. Rekers*
15. Counseling and Homosexuality   *Earl D. Wilson*
16. Counseling for Anger   *Mark P. Cosgrove*
17. Counseling and the Demonic   *Rodger K. Bufford*
18. Counseling and Divorce   *David A. Thompson*
19. Counseling and Marriage   *DeLoss D. and Ruby M. Friesen*
20. Counseling the Sick and Terminally Ill   *Gregg R. Albers*
21. Counseling Adult Children of Alcoholics
    *Sandra D. Wilson*

*(Other volumes forthcoming)*

VOLUME TWENTY

# Counseling
# the Sick
# and Terminally Ill

## GREGG R. ALBERS, M.D.

## RESOURCES FOR
## CHRISTIAN COUNSELING

General Editor

## Gary R. Collins, Ph.D.

WORD PUBLISHING
Dallas · London · Sydney · Singapore

**Library of Congress Cataloging-in-Publication Data**

Albers, Gregg R., 1955–
    Counseling the sick and terminally ill / Gregg R. Albers
       p.   cm.—(Resources for Christian counseling : v. 20)
    Bibliography: p.
    Includes index.
    ISBN 0-8499-0693-8
    1. Church work with the sick.   2. Sick—Pastoral counseling of.
   3. Church work with the terminally ill.   4. Terminally ill—Pastoral
counseling of.   I. Title.  II. Series.
BV4335.A43   1989
259'.4—dc20                                    89-33718
                                             CIP

*Printed in the United States of America*
9 8 0 1 2 3 9 AGF 9 8 7 6 5 4 3 2 1

# CONTENTS

# EDITOR'S PREFACE

MANY YEARS AGO I had a professional colleague who was a great inspiration to everyone he met. Consistently gentle and sincerely concerned about others, he radiated a love for people and a positive outlook on life. Everybody spoke well of him and he never seemed to criticize or complain.

But I have never met a man with more physical problems. His kidneys didn't work like they should, his body chemistry always seemed to be off balance, he had heart problems, and there had been so many operations on his body that he had lost count. (He thought the number was between thirty and forty.) Ill health forced him to retire early, just at the time when his career seemed to be "taking off." From his sick bed he would call people or write cheerful notes of encouragement, but he rarely mentioned the pain that was his constant companion. Like Paul the apostle, my friend did not lose heart in the midst of adversity (2 Cor. 4:16, 17). Though outwardly his body was wasting away, inwardly he was "being renewed day by day."

Perhaps most of us have met people who honestly face adversities and physical problems but who somehow are able to rise above the pain, avoid complaining, and become great encouragers to others. More often, sickness and approaching death plunge us into discouragement, frustration, anxiety, and anger. Even when we keep our minds on God's goodness and sovereignty, it never is easy to face the tension and turmoil of a body that is breaking down and moving—sometimes far too quickly—toward disintegration and death.

From his perspective as a physician, almost every day Dr. Gregg Albers observes the pain, the pathos, and the psychological pressures that come with physical illness. He has watched people react to their illnesses and has experienced the joy of seeing patients recover—some so completely that they develop a new zest for living. As a Christian doctor dedicated to bringing the latest in medical technology to the aid of his patients, Dr. Albers knows, too, that there is great need for spiritual counsel and sensitive caring in the midst of our "high-tech low-touch" society.

Initially, I had difficulty finding an author to write this book. One dedicated husband-wife team (both physicians) accepted the invitation to write but later felt the need to withdraw, in part because of the almost overwhelming pressures of their busy rural medical practice.

Later, when I was introduced to Gregg Albers and we talked about this book, it was clear that he too finds himself inundated by the needs of his patients. Once, after he had begun writing, the author had to put aside this manuscript for several weeks while he and his staff coped with a local epidemic of measles. As a highly experienced physician and medical director at a growing university, Dr. Albers is familiar not only with measles in college students, but also with the counseling issues that accompany serious physical illness and death. His experience and constantly expanding knowledge are reflected consistently throughout the pages that follow.

Like all other volumes in the Resources for Christian Counseling series, this book is intended to be practical and helpful. Written by counseling experts, each of whom has a strong Christian commitment and extensive counseling experience, the books are meant to be examples of accurate psychology and careful use of Scripture. Each is intended to have a clear evangelical perspective, careful documentation, a strong practical orientation, and freedom from the sweeping statements and undocumented rhetoric that sometimes characterize writing in the counseling field. Our goal is to provide books that are clearly written, useful, up-to-date overviews of the issues faced by contemporary Christian counselors—including pastoral counselors. All of the Resources for Christian Counseling books have similar bindings and together they are intended to comprise a helpful encyclopedia of Christian counseling.

Many counseling books focus on interpersonal conflict or emotions such as depression or anxiety. Until recently, however, few writers have dealt in depth with the psychological and spiritual issues accompanying pain, accidents, persistent illnesses, and the approach of death. Writing from the depths of his experience and from his awareness of the relevant contemporary literature, Dr. Albers has produced a volume that is both practical and sensitive. Illustrated by frequent case histories, interspersed with relevant references to the Bible, aware of the unique therapeutic role of the church, and built on a creative counseling model, this book can be helpful even to counselors who rarely see a physically ill person or who have little medical knowledge. Dr. Albers writes in language that is understandable and free of jargon, but his book reflects a professional competence that will be applauded by his medical colleagues. The author is aware of these colleagues and knows that they, too, need encouragement and counseling at times—especially when they are faced with difficult ethical questions like those discussed near the end of the book.

As you read the chapters that follow, I hope you will share my enthusiasm about Gregg Albers's contribution to this series of books. Now that his volume is finished, the doctor can be free to devote his energies to other writing projects—or perhaps to the next outbreak of measles!

*Gary R. Collins, Ph.D.*
*Kildeer, Illinois*

## PART ONE

# CARING IN TIMES OF SICKNESS

# CHAPTER ONE

## THE RESPONSE TO ILLNESS

Everything was going well for Nancy. At thirty-three years of age, she had all she desired—a loving Christian husband, a booming career as a seminar speaker, her own schedule—everything except a child.

Suddenly, she began to bleed excessively during her menstrual period. Pain and bleeding persisted for days until she became worried, weak, nauseated, and unable to work. When she consulted her family physician, he examined her thoroughly and sat her down to talk.

"Your uterus is filled with fibroids and probably should be removed," he solemnly suggested. "I know how badly you have wanted children."

3

After receiving the same opinion from a gynecological surgeon, she consented to the hysterectomy.

Just before surgery, Nancy started to lose weight. She grew weak, tired, and was subject to crying spells. When she awoke after surgery, she was sobbing and muttering: "My baby is gone! My baby is gone! My baby is gone!" During her hospital recuperation, she became hostile and confused while crying for "my baby." After a week, she was transferred to the psychiatric floor with psychotic depression.

It took months before she could be released from the psychiatric unit to finish recuperation at home. Nancy seemed to deteriorate whenever she looked at pictures of her family and at reminders of her childhood. Large doses of antidepressants barely helped her maintain any sense of reality. Even years later, she has never recouped the vibrant spirit she had before her hysterectomy. Her unstable mental condition has precluded an adoption—even though her psychiatrist and family physician both suggested caring for a child as the best therapy for her.

George was a relatively young man to own such an old body. Over the last ten years he had been stricken with high blood pressure, diabetes mellitus, strokes, heart attacks, hardening of the arteries, leg ulcers, and mild dementia. His faith, however, was unshakable through the testings of his physical illnesses. Emotionally, he was not anxious or angry about this rapid deterioration. He remained at peace, knowing that God was too wise to make a mistake.

When I saw George in the emergency room late one afternoon, he was short of breath and had massive amounts of fluid in his legs and abdomen. His severe chest pain was barely relieved by nitroglycerin. He was transferred immediately to the intensive care unit in severe pulmonary edema and further tests showed he had experienced a third heart attack. His heart was barely pumping blood. Without rapid improvement, he would soon be in heaven.

As before, George was at peace with the situation. "Do what you can," he said between gasps for air. We had discussed letting him go without "heroic" treatments, such as CPR or intubation, but his wife preferred to give him every chance to survive.

She suggested it was "the Lord's will" at this time. I agreed and we kept treating him aggressively.

Though George had less than one chance in a thousand of surviving severe heart failure on top of a third heart attack, he improved slowly, but surely, with medical therapy. He was only fifty-eight. We didn't want to let him go, but it was difficult to contend with his deteriorating body.

Silently, peacefully, George's emotional strength seemed to pull him further and further from death's door. He continued improving physically with the treatments we gave.

I can explain George's recovery from such dire medical problems only in emotional and spiritual terms. He had already accepted his medical problems cognitively and emotionally. His healing abilities were infused by emotional and spiritual maturity, leading to remarkable—almost miraculous—healing in his body.

Though he died later that year, he was granted eight wonderful additional months with his family. His spiritual maturation through the testings of illness was a great encouragement to family, to friends, and to myself, his physician.

## THE EMOTIONAL REACTION TO ILLNESS

The process of illness obviously involves more than a physical progression of symptoms from illness to resolution. It involves a highly integrated emotional structure that may become unbalanced and diseased as the patient loses balance in physical health. Emotional reactions are inseparable from the physical symptoms manifested during illness. But just as the body can heal many physical ailments without medical intervention, these same inborn processes can often restore psychological balance following illness, as we saw with George. An individual's spiritual maturity can deeply affect emotional and physical healing abilities.

At times, emotional reactions to illness may become more devastating than physical symptoms. The emotional state can prolong physical symptoms. Emotional reactions may be out of proportion to the severity of the physical illness. They may create extreme problems for the family that must deal with both the physical and emotional aspects of recovery. It is with these

5

"pathological" reactions to illness that the professional or lay counselor can begin ministry to patient and family.

Little has been written about emotional reactions to illness compared with the companion topic of emotional reactions to terminal illness and grief.[1] The patient's reactions to physical illness can best be described by the "grief reaction" model, which has been well described in the literature. It will be modified for specific differences between short-term illness and terminal illness. To better understand these reactions, we will consider a new model that combines classic grief models with the scriptural context for suffering and testing.

**The Grief Reaction**

Few people push themselves as hard as Samuel. He is a workaholic, a Type A personality, as compulsive and energetic as any man I know. Like all busy people, he hates any interruption in his busy schedule, especially personal illness.

The day he came to my office he was minimally concerned about his cough, which had persisted through three different courses of antibiotics. His exam was normal, but we decided to make sure that everything looked normal in his chest. We were shocked and distraught by what we found on his chest x-ray: a large mass in the middle of his lung. This was diagnosed after further x-rays and a biopsy as Hodgkin's lymphoma, a potentially fatal cancer. We scheduled surgery for early the next week.

If anyone has ever fought harder than Samuel to deny the presence of an illness, I would be greatly surprised. The initial phases of denial seemed endless.

"It just couldn't be anything serious because I have had a spot on my lung before."

"I have so many projects that need to be completed, I just don't have time for an illness."

On and on went the excuses and emotional confusion.

Mixed with the denial were many other defense mechanisms common in grief reactions. He had episodes of bargaining with God, when he would promise to slow down if God would heal the mass before surgery. Samuel tried to blame foreign travel and some exotic parasite as the real reason for the mass. He read article after article suggesting stress and immune-system changes as the cause of the tumor. He even rationalized that changing his lifestyle, reducing stress, and caring for himself better were all he needed.

Not until after surgery, numerous tests, and the beginning of radiation and chemotherapy did Samuel finally accept the disease as "his problem." Months elapsed, and his physical strength was almost gone, before he began to fully trust God through the testings of illness. Now, seven years after that initial diagnosis, the tumor has not recurred. Samuel is healed, and he has a ministry to those who also suffer with cancer.

After years of active medical practice, attending the needs of both the temporarily and the terminally ill, I have seen little difference between the emotional reactions of these two groups. The similarities far outweigh the differences. The range of psychological defenses used to stabilize the patient's self-esteem are identical when comparing the individual who has a temporary illness with one who is terminally ill.

This makes a great deal of psychological sense. The person with physical pain and altered function is initially confused and concerned. Will the pain increase? Will the disability get better or worse? Will other symptoms begin? Fears that he or she may die from this illness raise the same defensive reactions seen in all illnesses.

Lack of a specific diagnosis and the fear of increased suffering may lead temporarily to a confused psychological response. The series of defenses may involve denial alternating with rationalization or projection. Clear-cut progression from one stage of the grief process to the next does not occur until the patient knows and understands more specific information about the disease and prognosis.

Although the psychological reactions to illness are similar, whether temporary or terminal, modulating factors blunt the emotional trauma in temporary illness. An illness with few, nonsevere symptoms is less likely to raise fears of death. If the patient has already experienced a similar illness, psychological reactions have been rehearsed and he or she remembers the final outcome. A rapid diagnosis of the illness and reassurance of a benign condition help keep emotional trauma to a minimum. A

7

strong, supportive family member who remains at the side of the patient can soothe apprehensions and fears. A caring manner and knowledge of the illness can help the person withstand hysterical emotions. The same results can be gained from the physician-patient relationship when caring communication accompanies each step of testing and treatment.

Viewing physical illness as a spectrum, from minor physical ailments all the way to serious disorders resulting in death, can help us understand how emotional reactions to illness are similar, depending upon severity. Studies of the responses to illness suggest various components of the grief response. They include coping, vulnerability, and the reality defenses an individual uses to protect self-esteem.[2]

In a rare book devoted entirely to psychological processes involved with illness, Dr. Stephen Green sums up a chapter by saying,

> Whether impaired health is experienced in the literal sense as a result of clear limitations in physical functioning, or in the more abstract symbolic sense, it precipitates the same psychological response: illness is accompanied by a natural grieving process which is analogous to the grief reaction caused by the death of a loved one.[3]

As illness grows more severe, the patient becomes more vulnerable. Offensive and defensive weapons become more necessary to fight it. We all try to disarm the reality of illness by using reactional self-defenses, all of which follow the classic models for grief reactions.

## Classic Models of Grief

Grieving is a normal, natural process involving strong emotional response to loss. We experience it often during our lives— in times of sickness, in times of mourning, in times of conflicts that bring loss. We are no strangers to this process; and though it is unpleasant, we must all face its inevitability.

People have grieved for centuries. In ancient literature, however, the scientific study of grief receives only brief mention, despite abundant philosophical and religious notation. By contrast, Victorian literature is famous for its open philosophical discussions of many aspects of death.

Scientific interest in either the grieving process or the psychological condition of the dying individual was rare until the second half of this century. Case histories describing the psychodynamics of dying patients are relatively few, although Felix Deutsch, Eissler, Sanford, Joseph, and Norton have published descriptions of patients dying of cancer.[4] Freud and Eissler refer to the reluctance of being in contact with a dying person, which may be a factor contributing to the rarity of such case reports.[5] These researchers emphasized the significance of a psychotherapeutic attitude and the importance of better understanding the psychodynamics of the dying patient.[6]

It wasn't until 1969 that Elisabeth Kübler-Ross published *On Death and Dying*, a text that made the study of the grief reaction more popular. Her five stages of grief were derived from a composite study of about 200 dying patients. Each was interviewed extensively in order to discover reactions and coping mechanisms. These five stages have since become a standard for many who write on the subject.

Though not all patients move progressively through the stages, most exhibit psychological reactions to each of these areas. The first stage is denial and isolation. Here the patient's strongest weapon in fighting the shock of imminent death is to deny its reality and to avoid those who see it. The second stage is anger, the typical reaction of shaking a fist at God and saying, "Why me?" The third stage is bargaining, a feeble attempt to exchange the unpleasant fate for a better one. The fourth stage, described as depression or sadness, is the beginning of a realistic emotional response. The patient begins to see the reality of death. The final stage is acceptance—seeing reality for what it is.[7]

Other models for this grief process have also been offered, many similar to the Kübler-Ross progression, others demonstrating different understandings and purposes. J. R. Averill describes the grief process in three stages: shock, despair, and recovery.[8] Colin Parkes suggests four essential stages: numbness, pining, depression, and recovery.[9] Richard Kalish suggests that these three theories parallel one another.[10] Weizman and Kamm use the Kübler-Ross framework but attach different labels to each stage: shock, undoing, anger, sadness, and integration.[11] Worden believes stages give people "too literal" an understanding of the process, such as the "phases of Parkes." For him, the "tasks of mourning" description works better and refers to tasks that must be accomplished in a non-specific order.[12]

When Kübler-Ross discusses "the different stages that people go through when they are faced with tragic news—defense mechanisms in psychiatric terms, coping mechanisms to deal with an extremely difficult situation," she describes only common emotional reactions seen when traumatized people try to prevent pain.[13] Grief, as characterized by many experts, is not an orderly, stage-to-stage process. Some people may skip stages completely. Others may proceed rapidly to the fourth stage and then return to the second and third. Humans prove their adaptability in the grief process by using defense mechanisms learned from previous emotional traumas.

All patients can use these psychological mechanisms to help survive a painful grief ordeal. But the most mature apparently reject such crutches when dealing with personal death or illness. Do they have a special way of grieving? Have they already completed the grief process before becoming ill? Do they have special spiritual resources that others do not?

A theory of grieving should include even these special people who give comfort to others while they are dying. It should correspond to biblical principles and give spiritual comfort. It should help us understand illness and conflict, as well as death. Secular explanations of the grieving process lack an important element here. They approach it only briefly in humanistic or existentialistic terms. That missing element is the purpose of suffering, of grieving, of dying.

Though present theories are helpful and accurate in describing typical emotional reactions to illness and death, I would like to propose a composite theory of grief as a framework for our counseling strategies for the sick and the terminally ill. It is a theory based upon biblical principles, and it supports a strong purpose for suffering.

### THE UNIFIED THEORY OF GRIEF COUNSELING

The framework proposed here is a composite of many grief theories: Kübler-Ross's stage theory, Parke's phase theory, Hagglund's transactional theory, Worden's task-completion theory, and Bugen's predictive theory.[14] It takes the process further into the recovery, readjustment, or growth phases, however, lending a more noble purpose and scriptural basis to grief and physical suffering.

Grief can be described as a simple three-phase process. The first, the *reaction* phase, employs the usual defense mechanisms and sorting out of emotional confusion. This corresponds to stages one through four in the Kübler-Ross framework, phases one through three in the Parke framework, and three of the four tasks of mourning suggested by Worden. The physical symptoms of grief are also present during this phase.

The second phase is that of *acceptance.* Whether called acceptance, reorganization, recovery, or something else, the process is the same. The individual must finally admit the reality of the loss and grieve for it. At this point most secular counselors and therapists suggest termination of therapy. It is also the point of differentiation between normal and pathological grief. Normal grief moves without assistance through the reaction phase to the acceptance phase. Pathological grief persists in the reaction phase, heaping emotional pain upon pain and leading to depression, anger, and bitterness.

Acceptance includes two separate, but coherent, tasks: cognitive acceptance and emotional acceptance, both of which are necessary and interdependent.

The third, final, and most important phase in the Unified Theory of Grief is the *growth* or maturation phase. This focuses on the spiritual purpose of sickness, suffering, and dying. Yet it has been given only minimal mention in the secular literature. Kübler-Ross speaks rightly of the positive aspects of hope and its strengthening effects, physically and emotionally.[15]

In her book *Death: The Final Stage of Growth,* she and others speak in existential, metaphysical terms about the eternality of the soul and its place in history and the universe.[16] The psycho-analyst Hagglund suggests grieving and death coincide with a psychoanalytic pattern of personal growth.[17] Kalish takes the humanistic perspective that death is part of the evolutionary cycle of living.[18] Others also suggest some aspects of growth from the dying process, but all show less than an elevated Christian understanding.

### Spiritual Reasons for the Unified Theory

This theory simplifies the numerous scientifically based theories of noted psychologists and psychiatrists who study grief and dying. But it is also filled with strong spiritual implications for the Christian counselor or pastor. Designed around the very foundation of why suffering has been allowed by a loving God, a God who is greatly concerned about the welfare of each individual, the theory fulfills virtually all of the proposed psychological and theological reasons for suffering.

Christian theologians have written many excellent treatises seeking to answer the age-old questions of suffering and death. From Martin Luther to more contemporary thinkers such as C. S. Lewis,[19] the subject has been discussed and debated at length. Although we cannot examine each of these works, a review of Scripture will help us understand the positive uses God has for suffering.

Sickness and death are a normal part of living within a sinful world. The fact that our race has chosen to sin means that God has a loving obligation to restrict our sinful walk away from his care. Many Christians are disciplined, called to repentance, or receive salvation because of a physical ailment (Gen. 3:17–24; Ex. 15:26). Personal sin sometimes results in disease. But this is not always the case. Job's physical ailments were not because of his sin, nor was the man born blind because of sin (Job 2:1–7; John 9:2, 3). These conditions were simply to prove the faith of these men, bringing glory to God.

Imagine how few people would maintain a relationship with God in a world without disease or suffering. People would become sadly addicted to pleasure, to fulfilling their own lusts. Where need is strong, faith will grow.

If sickness, disease, suffering, and death are a normal part of living and have been allowed to exist by a loving God, what purpose is served by their presence in the lives of both believers and nonbelievers?

Suffering, above all, is a means God uses to show our mortality and need for him. He has allowed the most unpleasant of human circumstances, that of suffering, to encourage us to seek him (James 5:14–15). I can give example after example of patients who made a death-bed profession of faith or who were brought to the point of salvation by physical illness, emotional illness, or interpersonal conflict. Exodus 15:26, Psalm 119:71, and Isaiah 53:5 speak of both physical and spiritual healing.

Suffering not only can bring us to salvation. It also builds and matures the believer. Sickness can refine our faith (1 Pet. 1:5–7) and produce patience, perseverance, character, and maturity within us (James 1:2–4, Rom. 5:3–5, Heb. 12:11). It can conform us to the image of Christ (Rom. 8:28, 29 and 2 Cor. 3:18) and allow us to share in the suffering of our Lord (1 Pet. 2:18–24, 3:14–18).

Even the very act of grieving or mourning is encouraged because of its maturing effects on the griever. Grieving has a humbling effect on the believer (James 4:6–10). In the Sermon on the Mount, Jesus elevates grieving because it produces reliance upon God for soothing and comfort (Matt. 5:4). Christ himself was a man of sorrows, well acquainted with grief (Isa. 53:3). Scripture describes the grieving process as having a healing effect on the soul.

Thus Scripture suggests that God allows suffering for two major reasons: people are humbled so that they will turn to God for salvation, and believers grow into the image of Christ.

If the grieving process involves this high calling of God, shouldn't scientific observations of that process also correspond? Unfortunately, without a personal spiritual understanding of the outcome of grief, the unregenerate scientist cannot see its ultimate good. This is why secular theories stop at the acceptance stage, with only a few showing a hazy glimpse of the spiritual concept of growth.

Yet this is the basic purpose of the Unified Theory of Grief. It supports the positive aspects which the grieving process has for the individual. The physical benefits of acceptance and growth to the infirmed individual's immune system are provable and will be discussed later. We gain the emotional and spiritual benefits of the grief process through maturation—emotional maturation to handle losses and conflicts and spiritual maturation to conform us to the image of Christ.

## Spiritual Parallels

The Unified Theory of Grief produces interesting parallels with many aspects of the Christian life, especially the process of salvation and spiritual growth.

The reaction phase of the Unified Theory shows a human, emotional attempt to deal with losses. In the human sinful state, a person uses emotional rationalizations and reactions in his or her meager attempts to justify behavior. When the reality of physical infirmity begins to break through the psychological defenses, the individual comes to the point of emotional acceptance of the disease.

The same is true with our spiritual infirmities; we must put aside our human devices, accepting the sacrifice of the cross for our sins. Growth through our physical suffering brings us to emotional and spiritual maturity. Nonbelievers may grow emotionally, but they cannot understand how illness will deepen their faith and reliance upon God. Our reactions as Christians and our acceptance and growth through physical illness parallel our acceptance of Christ and our spiritual growth following salvation.

The same is true for emotional conflicts and interpersonal relationships. We often react to a situation through selfishness, anger, emotional outbursts, and pride, especially if we are on the losing end. Little progress comes until we accept the purpose and reality of the change, permitting further growth to occur in or through that relationship.

Conflict, pain, suffering, disease, and death are a necessary part of our maturation both as adult individuals and as believers. We will see these concepts more clearly as we discuss the Unified Theory of Grief and its parts in depth.

## The Reaction Phase

The spiritual perspective of grieving supports the contention that the purpose of suffering is to bring forth the fruit of maturity. Thus, the most important aspect has been forgotten or downplayed by those with only a secular understanding of grief. But how does the Unified Theory of Grief mesh with established, well-observed theories already in existence? We will begin by discussing the first phase of the grief process in depth, showing how scientific observation and theories also support this new framework.

The reaction phase is defined as the initial phase of the grief reaction when an event or illness triggers damaging emotional responses, psychological defenses, and physical symptoms. This is an involuntary response and each individual unconsciously uses the defenses and reactions that best suit his or her unique needs. Reason, knowledge, and maturity can modulate these emotional reactions.

The Lord created our bodies and minds to be so functionally integrated that when one area is diseased the whole becomes involved. The process of physical illness cannot be separated from its effect on the emotions. This is described as the psycho-biological balance.[20] The emotional complications of physical disease directly influence the patient's ability to recover. The movement from health to illness involves uncomfortable physical symptoms and many unpleasant psychological reactions. Whether involved with death or disease, physical suffering creates emotional reactions, the first phase of the grief response.

The reaction phase of the grief response occurs because patients experience actual or perceived losses in themselves or in family members. Loss can precipitate any or all of the reality defense mechanisms.

## Grief, Illness, and Losses

Anyone who experiences illness must adjust to losses. These include loss of control, time, function, a body part, a cherished role, self-esteem, family position, and income. The degree of loss depends upon the severity and course of the illness.

A prolonged or serious illness can result in *loss of control.* Patients are unable to keep their usual routines, perform normal activities, and make medical decisions affecting their care. They are often unable to communicate their confused feelings about the illness. This feeling of utter helplessness is frightening to almost everyone and can psychologically cripple those people whose abilities and work enable them to control everything and everybody around them. The more control individuals have over their jobs, families, and daily routines, the more damage the illness can do to their emotional stability.

Another loss of contemporary importance is the *loss of time.* No culture is as time-conscious and time-dependent as our materialistic Western society. Loss of a few days for surgery may be seen as loss of a contract, loss of a client, or loss of one's hard-earned position in the company. Time is money in our society. Disability doesn't pay—enough.

The *loss of function*—inability to walk because of a leg fracture, inability to breathe easily because of heart failure, inability to eat solid food because of a digestive problem, inability to perform sexually because of a prostate problem—each may cause great emotional turmoil. The patient asks many questions. Will my function return to normal? Will I always be handicapped? Will I be accepted by my family, my friends, or my colleagues if I am disabled? Will I be able to do my job?

*Loss of a part of the body* is always a shock. The loss of a breast to cancer, a leg to hardening of the arteries, a uterus and child-bearing ability—each of these pushes the patient through a grieving process. After resolving the grief the question remains, "How can I compensate for the lost part?" Many people recover physically through rehabilitation but are never whole emotionally.

Illness can cause the *loss of a cherished role*—in the family, in a peer-group, or in a professional situation. A woman loses the ability to be a mother, a role she desires more than career, more than money. A teenage leader in his church youth group must relinquish his position because of a six-month recovery from mononucleosis. A middle-aged man has to forfeit his seniority on the line because a heart attack has disabled him, allowing only a desk position. When sickness comes, one's cherished role, one's niche in society, his or her image of usefulness may be lost, and the ladder may have to be climbed all over again.

When a person loses or perceives a loss of control or of position or of function or of a body part, he or she suffers an inevitable *loss of self-esteem.* A positive attitude about recovery, a belief in one's ability to overcome present problems, is a key ingredient often forgotten in the healing process. Often, patients show physical signs of progress but deny it because they are not emotionally ready for recovery. The healing process is stifled when the question of "why me?" persists. The body's recovery is slowed by self-defeating emotions such as guilt, frustration, and anger. Only when the "whys" are answered, the frustrations calmed, and the feelings released, can the restored emotions aid the recovering body. The emotional damage caused by a physical disease has left many able-bodied victims permanently disabled.

Finally, the *loss of income,* often accompanied by the addition of horrendous medical bills, can have devastating effects on the psychological recovery of the patient. I had a young patient who could not get better from a simple viral infection. The stress of an auto accident, the bills that kept coming due, and the illness caused this patient to end up in the hospital. The added bills and continued pressure from work and creditors forced this young man to stay ill. To get well meant he would have to face his financial obligations—without excuse. If he remained ill, at least he had an excuse.

## LOSSES AND THE FAMILY

The physician often forgets that the entire family structure is involved in the reaction phase of grieving. Even counselors trained to see unhealthy processes in terms of family-based interpersonal relationships may treat only the most urgent, immediate needs of the counselee. When illness disrupts routine behaviors, however, families are often as psychologically affected as the patient. Counseling to meet family needs during illness requires understanding the physical, emotional, and interpersonal losses occurring in the home.

The grief process within the family depends upon a number of factors: which member is ill, the severity of the illness, the suddenness of the illness, the role the afflicted member filled, and the ways the family must compensate for its loss.

The hospitalization of a workaholic father, for example, may have little effect on daily family routines or on meeting the emotional needs of the children. On the other hand, hospitalization of the mother in this family may disrupt almost every

17

schedule in the household; it leaves physical and emotional needs unmet and creates much more emotional stress on all the nonafflicted members.

The other factors of *severity, suddenness,* and *role* interact with specific losses to create unique emotional situations in the family. Most extended families can cope and adapt to the slow changes in personality and memory of an early senile dementia. Minimal severity of a chronic degenerative illness in a person in the care-receiving role does not present a catastrophic change for a family. In contrast are the immediate changes in the family of a middle-aged mother, the primary caregiver, who is discovered to have an aggressive form of ovarian cancer. All aspects of family routine are shattered. The acute malfunction often leads to chronic peaks and valleys in physical and psychological condition and may keep this mother in a care-receiving instead of a care-giving role.

Just as the individual experiences losses, so does the family, but in different terms. Losses of function in the father may require the wife or teenage children to seek employment. This potentially destroys the mutual interdependence of a close-knit family unit. The loss of self-esteem resulting from a physical illness may lead to bitterness and anger in the ill person. Angry and hostile communication within the family may then worsen communication patterns. Hostility may increase and lead to emotional and physical abuse.

The eldest child or teen may assume care-giving responsibilities to compensate for the loss of a care-giving mother. The father may shift sexual affections away from his wife to a teen daughter in these situations. Or he may seek a sexual relationship outside of the home and, in so doing, place more responsibility upon this new teenage "mother."

Knowing the emotional needs of each family member, observing the changes in relationships, and counseling these individuals to understand, accept, and grow through these trials can mean healing to a family damaged by the losses of illness.

### Reactions and Defenses

The study of grief has primarily been a study of the reaction phase of the entire process. Freud was the first to publish his observations of mourning in 1917.[21] Many years later others followed, such as Lindemann, who observed and recorded the grief reactions of more than 100 families and published his work in 1944. In the late 1960s, a number of schema for the orderly progression of the grief process were offered (Kübler-Ross, Parke, Worden, Bowlby, and others). Each investigator interviewed people in mourning and identified various reactions, coping mechanisms, and defenses.

The primary, earliest defense grieving or seriously ill individuals use is denial. Denial is a defense mechanism because it shields the person from a painful reality, relationship, or loss. Every textbook dealing with the subject of grief, death, suffering, psychology, or psychiatry has exhaustive descriptions of its use in emotionally traumatic events.

Denial cannot persist in a normal grief response. Anger, bitterness, sadness, hysteria, crying, depression, despair, betrayal, loneliness, abandonment, and many other reactions surface. The grieving or ailing individual may seem confused, bouncing from emotion to emotion, unable to make decisions and on the verge of emotional collapse. The strength of these emotional reactions depends upon the closeness to the individual, the suddenness of the event, and the interdependence among the people involved.

Studying models for grief shows that these reactions are all part of the initial "prerecovery" or "preacceptance" phase. A continuum exists from denial to the acceptance phase, where emotional responses become stronger as defense mechanisms give way to reality.

Defense mechanisms are mental constructs that hide or soften painful thoughts. These include *denial,* not thinking of reality; *projection,* displacing our feelings onto another; *repression,* a subconscious mechanism that lets us selectively forget a situation; *suppression,* consciously pushing painful details out of remembrance; *rationalization,* constructing a new reality that fits our needs; and *reaction formation,* making us feel and act in ways opposite to the way we actually feel. Most of these are subconscious mechanisms that help soothe our hurting self-esteem.

In addition to these psychological reactions, physical symptoms also occur during the reaction phase.

## Physical Symptoms

Marilyn, a tall, thin woman in her early sixties, had just gone through the most difficult time in her life. It was just three years since her husband had asked for a divorce after almost thirty years of marriage. She had recently retired from the company that had employed her for almost twenty-five years. And now she had to bury her father and take over caring for her mother, an Alzheimer's patient. She had been blessed with remarkably good health, but she awakened one night with crushing chest pain, extreme shortness of breath, heaviness in the arms and legs, and pain in the left shoulder. She was immediately rushed to the hospital.

When admitted to the cardiac treatment room, her heart was racing at more than 200 beats per minute. She could barely talk, and was gasping for every breath. After initial treatments, tests, and oxygen, some of the symptoms started to slow. She was transferred to the coronary intensive care unit because the doctors feared a heart attack—the very thing that had killed her father. When they mentioned their concerns, the symptoms immediately got worse.

She was treated with painkillers and sedatives and became unconscious of what was going on around her. Within hours, she was much calmer. Repeated testing relieved the fears of heart damage. Eventually nothing was found, no hardening of the arteries, no damage to the heart, no lung problem, and no physical disease that could account for the seriousness of the episode Marilyn had sustained. The final diagnosis was severe stress reaction with hyperventilation.

Marilyn remained exhausted and depressed for weeks. Though she eventually recovered without further medication, no one expected these symptoms to last as long as they did.

Many authors and texts describe the physical symptoms associated with a grief reaction. It is important to understand the origin and constellation of these symptoms. They are often superimposed upon a preexisting physical problem. Many physicians overtreat an illness overlaid with grief symptoms only to find that the treatment makes the patient worse.

Erich Lindemann's 1944 article probably contains the best description of the classic physical symptoms of grief. These include wave-like episodes of tightness in the throat, shortness of breath, an empty feeling in the abdomen, a heaviness or numbness of the body, and a feeling of tension.[22] Worden included other symptoms in a study published in 1982: oversensitive reaction to noise, sense of depersonalization, lack of energy, muscular weakness, and dry mouth.[23]

Any physiology student will immediately recognize the source of these symptoms. Strong emotional reactions are tied to the autonomic (the automatic) nervous system through an area of the brain called the hypothalamus. The above symptoms are identical to the "fight or flight" response that causes automatic changes in bodily function whenever a person is threatened. Evidently, whenever someone remembers a loss, this evokes an emotional response that stimulates the autonomic nervous system. This stimulation causes these physical symptoms. This is what happened to Marilyn. A person may get the same symptoms when watching a frightening movie.

Chronic overstimulation of the autonomic nervous system through emotional channels will also result in more serious physical maladies. These are also seen in those who are chronically overstressed or persistently grieving. The symptoms result from the same autonomic hyperstimulation. They include headaches, dizziness, fainting, rashes, ulcers, irritable bowel disease, heartburn, vomiting, palpitations, chest pain, fatigue, panic attacks, and weakness.

Treatments for these specific symptoms should aim at the source of the problems—the emotional stimulation of the autonomic nervous system. Tranquilizing agents have an effect on the disorganization of grieving thoughts, and they slow the stimulation of the autonomic nervous system. Antidepressants can lessen chronic overstimulation by restoring a biochemical balance to the overloaded hypothalamus. Of course, counseling a patient to understand and accept the reality of the disease, and to complete the grieving process, are the ultimate reasons for this book and will be discussed throughout the remaining chapters.

The reaction phase of the grief process is a well-known and well-studied entity. It is precipitated when illness or loss initiates coping mechanisms and psychological defenses to protect the individual from emotional pain. As the defense mechanisms fade and reality becomes more visible, the strength of the emotional responses and physical symptoms increases (Figure 1). The reaction phase ends only when the grieving or ill person can *accept* the reality of loss and begin the climb into the *growth* phase of the process.

### The Acceptance Phase

Emotional resolution begins with acceptance of the disease or loss. To reach this point in the grief resolution process, the patient must complete two primary tasks. First, the patient must cognitively understand what the disease is and how it should be treated. Second, he or she must emotionally accept the reality and discomfort of the disease and then accept responsibility for future treatments and the outcome.

The patient must understand the cause of the disease, the course of the disease, the best treatment (surgery or therapy), and its likely outcome. They may not understand the spiritual

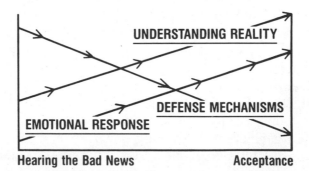

**Figure 1** When a patient hears the bad news of his or her loss, the defense mechanisms are strongest. Emotional responses are minimal, and a sense of the reality of the loss is also minimal. Later, the patient understands more about the illness and often becomes more emotional. Defense mechanisms become less able to postpone reality and are less useful. When a patient accepts loss, a sense of reality is high and the use of defenses is low.

purpose of illness because they cannot accept a disease that will never fit their expectations. Some may remain angry with the physician or the nursing staff. Some may rebel against rational treatments and refuse proper medication.

During the course of an emergency hospitalization for a stroke, the wife of an elderly man became quite irate with the physician and nurses. Her husband had improved quickly and was even regaining his speech. The physician expressed pleasure with his rapid progress and assured the wife that her husband would have few, if any, losses in physical function or speech.

Three mornings later, the patient suffered a second stroke. Though the episode was obvious to the nursing staff, the wife misunderstood. She perceived this as negative progress and became frustrated and agitated at the physician, rationalizing that this decline was due to a change in medication. Over the next week, the wife became upset with all aspects of his care. Another physician was called in to review the situation and help the wife understand what had happened.

"If they had only been more realistic at the beginning, I would have been able to accept his deficits. I feel like I have been lied to," the wife explained. She did not understand the course of this malfunction and was unwilling to accept the disease and her losses.

The physician must give a thorough, proper explanation of the disease, its course, and prognosis in order for the patient and family to cognitively understand and eventually accept the illness. Miscommunications and misunderstandings unfortunately are common with the increasing sophistication of modern medicine. But if our patients do not understand, they may delay acceptance and stall their healing process.

Too often we counsel a family to accept the emotional realities of grief only to find persistent anger over how or why their loved one actually died. Just as children find and hold firm to any unfairness in a parent's discipline, so patients stay bitter and angry if an illness dealt them seems unfair. Herein lies a great ministry for the Christian counselor and pastor who, like the patient, understands the concept of disease on a less complex level. They can help convey a cognitive understanding of the disease process to these grieving individuals.

The ultimate goal is to attain cognitive and emotional acceptance of the patient's condition. Acceptance is the key to unlocking the healing powers within and to returning from slow self-destruction to new levels of spiritual maturity.

## Acceptance: Return from the Valley

Why is it so important for our grieving patients to accept their losses? Why is acceptance, resolution, or recovery touted in secular theories of grief as the ultimate recovery point?

Leonard A. sustained a severe heart attack and was recovering in the coronary intensive care unit. He was bitter and angry with his wife over the series of fights they had had the past few weeks. He blamed her for his obesity, his drinking binges, and his smoking habit. When his physician told him he could never smoke again, the nurses had to cover their ears to avoid the extremely loud, vulgar language of reprisal.

This patient's progress was very slow. He never went back to work. He continued to fight over senseless situations at home, and he would curse the physician under his breath every time he lit a cigarette. He died three months later of another massive heart attack.

Leonard B. also sustained a severe heart attack, but he grieved about his lifestyle, smoking, and poor eating habits. His arguments with his wife suddenly ceased as he realized his life was near its end. He regretted not spending more time with his children and grandchildren.

This patient's progress was almost miraculous. He went back to work in just four weeks. He stopped smoking and enrolled in a walking and diet plan. His attitudes changed dramatically toward his wife and family. When his heart was checked a year after his heart attack, only a small amount of permanent damage was found. The physicians had expected the entire front wall of the heart to be damaged, but found most of it functioning normally.

From a physical standpoint, Leonard A. and Leonard B. had almost identical heart attacks, but their outcomes were completely different. Many cases of almost miraculous recoveries from trauma, diseases, cancers, and arthritis have been recorded and in each the patient's attitude has had a positive effect on healing. Every physician I know has seen a few patients like Leonard A. and a few more like Leonard B. The acceptance of disease and the resultant change in attitudes are considered a "cure" to physicians and mental health professionals alike.

It can be helpful to look at the positive and negative effects grieving emotions have on the body's healing mechanisms. The negative effects are clear. In 1987, *The American Journal of Psychiatry* reported:

> The last decade has produced a series of studies which indicate that psychological stress and psychiatric illness can compromise immunologic function. Hence, these studies suggest the psychological state will influence susceptibility to illness and/or its course and prognosis.[24]

The immune system, the cells that defend the body from infectious disease and repair and heal damaged tissues, is the system affected by positive or negative emotions. The persistent effects of denial, bitterness, grieving, anger, and depression have been shown in numerous cases to decrease the body's ability to heal. This corresponds to clinical psychological assessments that demonstrate grieving emotions perpetuate disease and infirmity.

How do these negative emotions affect the body? They cause excessive stimulation of the autonomic nervous system and excessive secretion of stress hormones. These, in turn, reduce the effectiveness of certain cells within the immune system. Research studies show that certain emotions impede the immune system's ability to function.[25]

Unfortunately, the converse is very difficult to study—that Leonard B. actually healed better because of his positive attitude. A few studies have shown the healing effects of certain hormones secreted during such activities as running.[26] Many anecdotal reports have also been published showing that positive emotions and attitudes increase one's chances of healing; one of the better-known such reports is the book by Norman Cousins, *Anatomy of an Illness*.

It appears that the goal of acceptance has strong physical and emotional benefits. As we counsel our patients to deal with their defense mechanisms, emotional reactions, sorrow, and depression to the point of acceptance, we help them restore stifled healing abilities. Resolving emotional suffering restores the patient to a normal range of emotional responses to relationships and life stresses. Acceptance becomes the nadir, the low ebb, where the immune system becomes reenergized and able to complete the healing process. The damaging emotions are put aside in favor of reparative ones. This is the upward, healing slope for which we strive as counselors (Figure 2). Those who are climbing out of the valley find the ascent to be a growing and maturing time in their lives.

### The Growth Phase

"Each time I get sick I look at Jesus and ask, 'Is it time yet?'"

Margie was a dear friend and a patient of mine. She had severe asthma and was maintained on at least two medications at a time. Occasionally she would have a severe attack, requiring hospitalization in the intensive care unit for days. Breathing treatments, intravenous medications, and sometimes a ventilator were necessary to keep her alive.

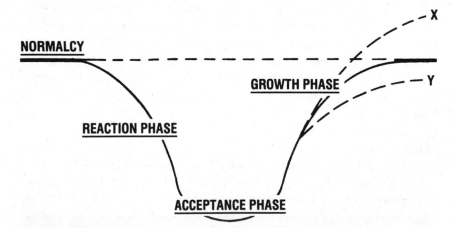

**Figure 2** During the descending period or reaction phase, physical and emotional declines occur until the patient reaches the low ebb of the acceptance phase. Then a reversal comes. In the ascending period of the growth phase, physical health and spiritual strength increase. Recovery occurs when the patient returns to normal physical activity and emotional stability. The dotted line "x" suggests the patient can recover and improve beyond his or her usual capabilities. The dotted line "y" represents a patient who has some disability and cannot return to normal function.

When she recovered between episodes, I could barely tell that she was so sick.

One rainy evening, she called saying, "Meet . . . (gasp) . . . me . . . (gasp) . . . at the . . . (gasp) . . . hospital!" I knew this was a bad episode. After a few breathing treatments and medications, she was able to breathe a little better. We hospitalized her in the ICU to watch her closely.

"I have always accepted my problem, and I have never gotten angry or bitter," Margie said. "In fact, I trust God so much more because of my asthma than before. I have to trust him because there is nothing I, or you doctors, can do when it gets that bad."

Her face beamed with confidence as she talked, which made me know she really did trust God for everything.

"Having a bad lung problem like asthma has made it possible for me to be nine-tenths in heaven already. I am looking forward to seeing his smile, and hearing his pronouncement 'Asthma: all healed.'"

Before another twenty minutes had passed, she had shared the gospel with three of the nurses and had them read a few Scriptures as she explained the love of God to them. They always loved to take care of her—she was such a pleasant, caring person.

I was called back to the ICU later that night. All of the nurses were crying, and so was I. Margie had quietly stopped breathing and even the respirator could not keep her on earth. Many grieved her passing.

I do know two who didn't cry—Margie and Jesus.

How do psychologists and psychiatrists explain those people who never grieve as they are sick or terminally ill? Does the person grieve if there is no sign of denial, bargaining, or sadness? Is it possible for acceptance to occur prior to the illness? What is God's reason for allowing suffering and grief if he does not mean it for our ultimate spiritual good?

Secular scientists who study the grieving process seek to ease emotional distress by teaching and counseling patients to understand and accept their circumstances. Christian counselors should immediately see this as an incomplete paradigm. Scripture and common sense help us see acceptance as the beginning of a long, fruitful growth phase. Patients are just beginning to benefit from their pain when secular psychologists brand them "healed." We can have the privilege of counseling them well into this growth phase if we see the ultimate goal of "Christlikeness" for our patients and ourselves. It is a form of discipling.

James speaks specifically of the growth phase in his first chapter. He calls his born-again brethren to see the trials and testings of life, the problems, the sorrows, the grieving, the pain, as "pure joy." He does not mean this in the masochistic understanding of pain for pain's sake. But he shows us the steps out of the valley. Testing of faith leads to perseverance. Perseverance leads toward maturity, toward the image of Christ. Each time we are tested, we have a choice—develop a deeper faith or complain, gripe, and get bitter. If we allow testings to increase our faith, we are more able to persevere through other trials as they come. The more we are able to persevere, the more mature we become.

Emotional growth and personal maturity are also byproducts of testings. Dr. Kübler-Ross suggests that even in the process of dying and death there is something more.

> That something else, that many can't define, is growth— becoming all that is truly you and at the same time, more fully human.[27]

Patients who have recovered from the brink of death develop new, more loving attitudes toward family, friends, and coworkers. The husband who almost loses his wife to illness no longer is gruff and demanding, but more helpful and kind. A child who grieves the loss of a parent can become an effective counselor for a friend who suffers a death as well. Dispositions, attitudes, personalities, and relationships all change because emotional maturity has resulted from a painful situation. Physicians, psychiatrists, psychologists, and pastors see these changes often, yet science has never taken an interest in studying the positive effects of suffering.

Maybe the following patients can demonstrate it more clearly.

Sandy, a thirty-two-year-old housewife with four kids, had a husband who was almost killed in a car accident. She said:

I just don't know how I made it. I know it must have been the prayers of our church, and God's Holy Spirit saying softly and quietly, "Hang on just a little longer."

Those three months when Gerald was in a coma were the worst. I couldn't rely on him for anything—not even to open his eyes and say with his smile, "I'm with you. I still love you." That's when I began to look to God to fill that void.

Now I know I can trust God in everything. In fact it wasn't until I had given Gerald up for dead and completely trusted in God for my needs, that he started to improve. When I walk, I now see his [God's] footprints next to mine.

Thomas, a sixty-four-year-old retired railroad engineer, lost his wife after a two-year bout with breast cancer.

One time when I saw Mimi cringe with pain, I just looked up at God and said, "I hate you for allowing this." Then Mimi squeezed my hand and said softly, "He is the One who is helping me." All of a sudden, I could release my anger and pain over my wife's cancer. It no longer seemed unfair. I just stood there and cried and hugged her.

God's love was never so real to me as the hour before Mimi died. It was like I knew that she was going to a place far better than here, where there was no pain. I felt a great relief was about to happen. It seemed too perfect to be true. The look on her face just before she died was one of joy and peace. It confirmed what my heart felt.

Margarite is a thirteen-year-old who has malignant melanoma.

At first, I didn't understand what "malignant" meant. Then as it started to spread to the bones of my arms and legs and started to hurt so much, I understood. But there was nothing to do except cry and pray.

The stories about Paul and his "thorn in the flesh," about the woman who was bleeding for eighteen years, and about Tabitha, who died and was raised by Christ, let me see how disease is a gift of God. In our pain, he gives us the gift of comfort. In our sadness, he gives the gift of joy. In our hopelessness, he gives the gift of hope.

I've been told there is no hope. But I told them his name was Jesus, and they just looked at each other. No one can take my hope away from me—no one.

In each of these patients, it is easy to see the emotional maturity and spiritual growth that resulted from their suffering. This book focuses on helping professional and lay counselors deal effectively with all three stages of the grieving process. It is important to gain skills and insights to help patients move through the reaction phase and the acceptance phase, and to be maintained in the growth phase. In setting our goal of treating distraught patients, we should not seek merely to alleviate unpleasant emotional reactions. We should want to help patients gain maturity and spiritual strength through the trials of affliction. Our calling is to minister just as Jesus did, by offering emotional and spiritual healing.

One other aspect of growth is seen in those who are physically ill but not seen in those who are terminally ill. This is the aspect of physical growth, restoration, and recovery.

## PHYSICAL GROWTH THROUGH ILLNESS

Try to put yourself in the place of a fifty-six-year-old man who has just suffered a heart attack. What might he be thinking?

"What am I going to be able to do once I am well? Can I exercise, can I work, can I have normal relations with my wife? How can I compensate for my problem? What kinds of conditioning or exercises are safe to improve my heart? What are my friends going to think? How will they treat me at the football games or at work? How am I going to survive all these changes in my life?"

The emotional trauma, the confusion, the doubts, and the fears all come because of a small blood clot that happened to hit the wrong artery. Hopefully this patient will be able to answer these questions by taking a step of faith—accepting this situation as God's will. The integral parts of this patient's acceptance and later growth are the tasks of physical *reassessment, goal setting,* and *recovery* of function. It is impossible to accept the diagnosis when even the physician does not know it. It is hard to set goals toward recovery when you don't even know where to start.

Once our patients have reached the level of cognitive and emotional acceptance of their diseases, they begin an ordered process of growth. This starts with the reassessment of physical abilities. It is stretched to intermittent and achievable goals and it culminates with a recovery of near-normal, normal, or increased function.

The realistic reassessment of a person's physical abilities allows him or her to establish workable goals and to keep self-motivated during rehabilitation. This personal reassessment of physical abilities, along with the physician's explanation of the probable course and treatment of the illness, allows the patient to build hope in the future, hope for returning to normal. If our patients' reassessments are based on an unrealistic estimate of their abilities, they are setups for failure, recurrent denial, and relapse into the reaction stage of grief.

The counselor can help make a realistic assessment of physical abilities by offering a more objective view of the situation; he or she can give realistic encouragement for improvement and energized hope for future restoration. A counselor can convey a more realistic view to patients with too rosy or gloomy an assessment by asking directed questions about abilities. "What specific things can you lift: a sack of fertilizer, a typewriter, a family Bible, or just a can of soda? How much activity does it take to make the pain return: simple walking, bending, jogging, or lifting a box? If you can walk without pain at home, why do you think walking at work causes pain?" Specifics will help increase the patients' perception of their present problems and their future recovery.

Goal setting is also essential for the rehabilitation of any person, especially one with chronic illnesses. Reachable goals act as benchmarks for improvement, "rest stops" along the way toward recovery. They help keep the patient motivated toward a seemingly unreachable goal, that of returning to completely normal function. Charts and graphs are excellent tools in showing self-improvement. Improvement is infectious. It breeds a positive attitude that motivates further improvement in both patient and family.

A counselor involved with reassessment and goal setting during an illness becomes an invaluable source of accountability afterward as well. Many families cast a dependent, nonimproving sick member in helpless roles that fulfill certain unmet psychological needs of other family members. The accountability of a professional counselor gives the patient more reason to continue with rehabilitation and less reason to remain in the sick role.

Some patients may resign themselves to not improving beyond a certain point. This can result in misinformation ("Uncle Bob just never got back to work after his hernia operation") from disabled friends or family who discourage full recovery. The counselor can establish the physical and emotional benefits of rehabilitation clearly, helping the patient achieve short-term and long-term goals. A counselor may be the most effective person to cheer a patient toward recovery.

The physical growth stage becomes final when patients recover most physical skills and strength, learn to compensate for losses, or improve to a condition better than before the illness. Most patients will recover from most illnesses. A few will not recover, but will find new ways to adapt present abilities to accomplish the same tasks as before. Stroke victims, for example, may not be able to write legibly but they may learn to type and circumvent the disability. A very few will use illness as a stepping stone to even greater achievements. One young man attempted to run across Canada after cancer resulted in the amputation of his leg. A Chicago executive ran his first marathon after a heart attack. Many other lives demonstrate these extremes of courage and discipline, all of which began with acceptance and growth from an illness.

One major stumbling block to our patients' resolution of the reaction phase of their grief is a lack of understanding of the disease, its consequences, its course, its treatment, its individuality, and its recurrence. In our increasingly complex medical environment, patients will be looking toward the physician, the professional counselor, or the pastor for understanding about their illness. Part of our ministry will be to make the complex simple so that our patients can understand their diseases, accept them cognitively, and eventually, accept them emotionally as well.

# CHAPTER TWO

# UNDERSTANDING ILLNESS

"What do you mean I'm not going to die from my cancer?"

Robert was an eighty-year-old lay evangelist, a dear saint of God. He had completed only a sixth-grade education, yet he seemed filled with the spiritual wisdom of Solomon and the zeal of Paul. Few believers could convey their desire to serve Christ as effectively as he. Though his appearance was rough and rugged, he was one of God's rare and beautiful gems.

Yet his question stunned me. He sounded disappointed.

"What do you mean? Is this cancer going to kill me or not?" Robert asked again.

"Illness is a highly complex process," I told him. "A myriad of variables may positively or negatively influence the outcome of your prostate cancer.

"For instance, your body's complex immune mechanism is adapting and fighting this foreign tissue in your prostate gland. But it needs the help of your digestive tract for proper nutrition. It needs your lungs and heart to supply oxygen, and it needs many other systems in your body to adjust to the changes.

"The cancer is quite variable as well. The older you get, the slower it grows. The cancer may spread to your bone, lungs, and brain. Or it may grow into the bladder and surrounding structures. The type of cell is the major determining factor in the aggressiveness of your cancer.

"Besides, you have a number of other health problems—heart disease, atherosclerosis, and hypertension—that are likely to claim you first. The prostate cancer probably won't lead to your death," I finished.

"Brother, you don't have to beat around the bush," he responded. "I'm ready to go home to Jesus. I just want you to be the prophet and tell me how soon."

## THE PROCESS OF DISEASE

In our world of instant diagnosis, prescriptions over the phone, and immediate Big-Mac Attack gratification, few patients take time to understand the complex, ever-changing process of health and illness. Too many people perceive health as a one-dimensional, static situation. Health is either good or bad. If it's bad, it needs to be fixed. Everyone hopes for that magic "fix-it elixir," which cures instantly with one great-tasting spoonful. But this is just not medical reality.

Each illness is as individual as the patient who contracts it. Each follows a progression of stages. The beginning stage of illness, the *incubation period*, starts and finishes before a patient knows a disease is present. The *symptomatic stage* produces changes in the body that are specific to one disease or a group of similar diseases. This is when a diagnosis is first entertained and when attempts are made to prove it. The *resolution stage* depends upon the body's healing mechanisms and any medications or therapies used to hasten return to normal function. The course of the resolution phase, and the effect of certain remedies and treatments, refine and confirm the diagnosis. The *recovery phase* replenishes the body's disease-fighting function so that future attacks can be thwarted successfully. Even after symptoms are resolved, the body continues recovering.

When we view the time line of a person's life, we see that illnesses are relatively short-lived changes superimposed upon the process of birth, growth, maturation, and degeneration. Illnesses affect these vital processes in major or minor ways. This is shown for three different patients in Figures 3, 4, and 5.

## Homeostasis

The concept of homeostasis is central to understanding the process of life. It is a concept promoted by American physiologist Walter B. Cannon, who suggested that the body maintains a stable, balanced internal environment through the operation of carefully coordinated functions.[1]

Temperature regulation is a simple example of this concept. The body attempts to maintain a balanced temperature of 98.6 degrees Fahrenheit. It produces heat by burning food and by muscle activity; heat escapes through the skin and through exhaled air. If the temperature drops, the body senses this heat loss and causes the muscles to shiver. This creates heat and restores homeostatic balance. When the body gains heat through exercise, the skin opens pores and increases perspiration to let it escape and again achieve a homeostatic balance. Because heat is constantly being produced and lost to the environment, the body makes minor adjustments each moment to preserve this delicate balance.

Why must natural systems maintain a balance? Because sickness comes when the balance is disrupted and when healing mechanisms become overwhelmed by infection, degeneration, or malfunction. The body increases repair efforts until the balance is again restored.

Healing is essential for life. Sickness is a loss of balance that occurs when destruction overwhelms healing. Death is the lack of healing. Without the ability to fight infection, a death from simple infections takes only hours, a few days at most. This has been scientifically documented in those born without immune function, those who lose function through cancer treatment, and those who lose function because of the AIDS virus.[2] To survive, the body must be able to heal itself.

35

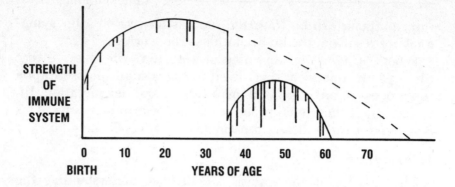

Figure 3   This lifeline represents a patient who contracted leukemia at age 35. It demonstrates years of declining immune strength after the illness, which hastened her death. The short vertical lines represent minor illnesses (colds, flus, etc.).

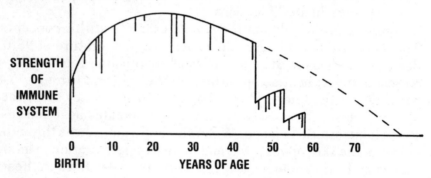

Figure 4   This lifeline represents a patient who sustained three separate heart attacks, beginning at age 45. The last heart attack caused his death. The short vertical lines represent minor illnesses.

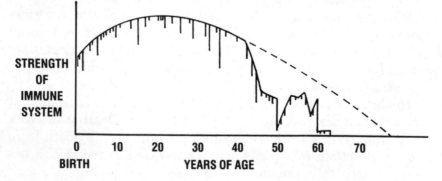

Figure 5   This graph represents the lifeline of a woman striken with lupus erythematosus at the age of 42. She had a heart attack at age 50, a stroke at age 60, and a second fatal stroke at age 62. The short vertical lines are minor illnesses.

Remaining in the reaction phase of the grieving process because of illness tends to hinder a patient's healing capabilities. Attitudes toward the cause of the illness and its outcome have great bearing on physical aspects of healing. This is why counselors can play a major role. They can help patients replace denial, anger, bitterness, and depression with a cognitive and emotional acceptance of their illness. This develops spiritual maturity, emotional resolution, and physical healing.

A counselor must understand the process of disease and healing to help patients understand. Even on a simple level, this will allow them to fully enter the acceptance and growth phases.

## THE PROCESS OF HEALING

Randy had been in the hospital only three hours when he became extremely short of breath. Diagnosed as having lobar pneumonia, he was started on intravenous antibiotics. During our initial talks, he admitted to drinking quite heavily. In fact, he had not stopped drinking for three consecutive weeks. Now he lay at death's door.

A tube was quickly placed in his lungs, and machines pumped life-preserving oxygen into his body. Since he had no strength to fight the pneumonia, it took three weeks before he could be taken off the ventilator.

Why had he deteriorated so rapidly? His immune system was destroyed by drinking. In addition to antibiotics and the ventilator, Randy's body demanded vitamins and minerals that drinking had depleted. His twenty-seven-year-old body was more fragile than many eighty-year-olds.

We have all heard of people with immune systems so destroyed by AIDS that simple infections can devastate once healthy bodies and minds. Many can recall accounts of the "bubble boy," the child born with no immune system, susceptible to a similar fate.

On the molecular and cellular level, each cell has the ability to reproduce, to resist invasion from toxins and bacteria, and to repair itself when damaged. This is part of the cell's design; protective instructions issue from the DNA in the cell nucleus. If a foreign invader attacks, the cell wall resists and protects it from penetration. Many cells can surround the offender, enclose it with a cell wall, and inject enzymes to dissolve and digest the particle. Each cell can sense destruction of a part of itself and repair it through DNA instructions and protein assemblers.[3]

The immune system is a collection of parts—lymph nodes, bone marrow, white blood cells, liver, spleen, skin, mucous membranes, etc.—that works in a highly coordinated fashion to prevent invasion by infectious agents and to repair any damage. Some white blood cells find, identify, and resist infectious agents. Others collect information and send chemical messengers to tell other white blood cells where to go. These other, specialized, "killer cells" seek out, surround, and destroy the infectious agents. This cell-to-cell communication occurs without any input from the nervous system. The immune system is a separate, self-controlled unit to keep the entire body free from damage.

At the first signs of an infectious agent, the immune system initiates the inflammatory response. Granulocytes, blood cells that release destructive chemicals around the infectious agent, also cause swelling, redness, and pain in the surrounding tissues. Without granulocytes, infections can spread far and wide with few signs or symptoms. Sometimes white blood cells release too much of a chemical, such as histamine in allergies, causing the person to suffer greatly. These same over-zealous cells can mistake normal tissue for foreign tissue, (such as the joint tissue in rheumatoid arthritis) and actually attempt to destroy it.[4]

An interesting spiritual parallel can be drawn between the body's response to infection and the purpose of suffering. The presence of infection without white blood cells would lead to a progressive, silent takeover of the area. The white blood cells create painful conflict as they try to rid the body of disease, conflict that causes redness, swelling, and increased temperature. But suffering results from the conflict—the effort to return to homeostatic balance—not from the infectious agent directly. The body's effort creates its own suffering.

No one enjoys suffering, but all pain proceeds from the process of returning an unhealthy state to healthy balance. Many Christians have written about the necessity, usefulness, and corrective power of pain. Dr. Paul Brand studied people who had leprosy for many years and found that much of the damage to the extremities was not due to the bacterium eating away at the tissue. It came instead from the absence of pain in hands and fingers, toes and feet.

"The gradual loss of the sense of pain leads to misuse of those body parts most dependent on pain's protection," Brand wrote. "A person uses a hammer with a splintery handle, does not feel the pain, and an infection flares up. Another steps off a curb, spraining an ankle, and, oblivious, keeps walking. Another loses use of the nerve that triggers the eyelid to blink every few seconds for lubricating moisture; the eye dries out, and the person becomes blind."[5] Pain is essential for physical preservation; suffering is essential for spiritual preservation.

A second spiritual parallel can be seen in the various functions of the immune system: reproducing cells, repairing damage, and restoring normal function. These properties match the innate emotional and spiritual healing abilities of the human mind and soul. Numerous well-known texts describe psychological defenses and mental reactions that either return an individual to health or persist as an inappropriate adaptation to a problem.[6] The human organism possesses an innate drive to return itself to "homeostatic" or "psychobiologic balance."[7] The normal grief response allows a person to react to problems, gently come to understand the reality of his or her losses, and then to accept them and grow in maturity.

God uses this same healing pattern in the spiritual life of believers. The Holy Spirit fulfills the role of the "spiritual immune system." He gives us the ability to reproduce through witnessing, the ability to discern when sin causes damage, and the understanding and motivation to regain normal spiritual function. At the center of God's very nature is the ministry of healing and restoration (Mal. 4:2; Ex. 15:26; 2 Kings 20:5; Ps. 103:3, 107:20; Isa. 53:5; Hos. 6:1; Matt. 10:8; Luke 4:18, 23, 10:9; Rev. 22:2).

Other than diagnosis and treatment of a given disease, the greatest ministry I have with my patients is teaching—teaching the causes and the course of the problem. When patients understand how the disease makes them ill, they have the intellectual tools to fight back. Most must learn to give up

39

their one-dimensional, static view of health before seeing the full, multi-dimensional view—the process of disease. Disease is not the black-and-white photograph we envision in our minds. It is a series of vivid, complex, ever-changing pictures, much like a color movie.

## THE PROCESS OF ILLNESS

This transformation of health into illness varies with the disease. The type of illness determines its course, symptoms, and outcome. The mechanisms of destruction vary, and their effect on organs and tissues does, too. Each illness is as different as the person who contracts it.

We can divide disease into three general categories for our understanding: infectious invasion, organ malfunction, and degeneration.

### Infectious Illness

The most commonly understood disease process is that of an infectious agent invading the body. Ever since the discovery of microbes in the eighteenth century by Anton van Leeuwenhoek and others, many people have believed that all disease is caused by external, evil forces or by microbes that invade, destroy, kill, and maim.[8] Although our understanding of disease has broadened and been refined, a large percentage of patients still act as if this were the exclusive concept of disease. I see this daily in my practice: patient after patient requests an antibiotic for a disease that is not infectious. This is one reason why we have become such a pill-oriented society.

Infectious invasions come from viruses, bacteria, fungi, and many different parasites. Generalized fever, local heat, redness, swelling, collections of "pus," and pain are the most commonly occurring symptoms. Infectious diseases follow the classic four-part process: an *incubation* period without symptoms; a *symptomatic* period; a *resolution* phase, during which the symptoms decrease under treatment; and a *recovery* phase, in which the body restores its immune reserves. The defenses are often lowered by stress, overwhelmed by too many bacteria, or broken by such causes as a cut in the skin.

Infections produce most of the world's illnesses—including

malaria, parasites, worms, influenza, colds, and all bacterial infections.[9]

Mononucleosis is an excellent example. Caused by the Ebstein-Barr (EB) virus entering the respiratory tract of a susceptible person, mononucleosis often occurs when tiredness, stress, or other infections have compromised the immune system. A large transfer of the virus occurs during kissing, thus lending its outdated name of "kissing disease."

It takes approximately thirty days of incubation before symptoms of fever, tiredness, sore throat, and nausea first appear. As the disease progresses, the patient loses weight, becomes more tired, and may develop an inflamed liver and spleen. During the resolution phase, which may last as long as four to eight weeks, these symptoms slowly disappear and the patient slowly gains more energy. During the recovery phase, after symptoms have gone, the patient remains susceptible to other respiratory illnesses with symptoms that are often similar. It is rare to contract "mono" again, but many victims are likely to contract other infections within six months to a year after the bout with mono.[10]

The hallmarks of infectious diseases are the following:

1. An external, living, causative agent—such as a bacterium, virus, or fungus.
2. A course that follows the typical incubation, symptomatic, resolution, and recovery phases, with or without treatment.
3. An inflammatory response—with pain, redness, swelling, and increased temperature in some body part—that results from the attempt to rid the body of the infectious invader.

## Malfunctional Illness

Infections are illnesses from invasion. Diseases of malfunction occur because organs either fail or produce too much or too little of their product. The improper performance of these organs throws other systems out of balance and causes distress for the patient. Malfunctions encompass a wide range of illnesses that are often based on an individual's genetic makeup. The body's tendency toward malfunction is difficult to treat, often taking months or years of medication or therapy to correct. Physical malfunctions are often an ever-present problem.

Several examples illustrate the breadth of this class of illness.

Diabetes mellitus is a classic example of organ malfunction. The pancreas produces insulin, a hormone essential for minute-to-minute regulation of blood-sugar level. Without it, the body cannot absorb sugar and use it for energy. In diabetes, the pancreas produces too little insulin, causing the body to "starve" for lack of energy. The blood glucose builds up in the bloodstream and leads to dehydration and acidosis.

The malfunction of the pancreatic islet cells that produce insulin has a devastating effect on all bodily cells. Each cell deteriorates when deprived of glucose. The treatment requires injections to replace insulin and return blood sugar to normal levels.

Diabetes fluctuates during an individual's lifetime. The necessary amount of insulin varies. The malfunction, however, requires treatment for the rest of the patient's life.

Malfunctions may cause deficiencies, such as diabetes mellitus (insulin deficiency) and depression (neuro-hormone deficiency). They may also cause excesses of secretion, such as hyperthyroidism and ulcer disease. When the thyroid gland makes and secretes too much thyroid hormone, it adversely affects many bodily systems, especially the heart. Very rapid heart rate and severe anxiety are the result. Under the influence of the emotional centers of the brain, the stomach can secrete too much acid and destroy its own lining, causing gastritis and ulcerations.

The body also malfunctions when the immune system, mistaking its own tissues for a foreign invader, attacks and attempts to destroy them. Rheumatoid arthritis, for example, involves white blood cells and antibodies attacking the lining of the joint, causing redness, swelling, pain, and inflammation. The disease waxes and wanes with the strength of the immune system, but untreated it ultimately leads to a stiff, non-functioning, painful joint many years later.[11]

Organ malfunctions can cause catastrophic illness, such as the severe situation of ketoacidosis in diabetes; or they can cause slow, long-term, low-level disease, such as high blood pressure. The excessive narrowing of the arteries causes the pressure in all the vessels to rise and puts a strain on the heart. This creates hardening and tears in the vessel lining, and sometimes causes bleeding in the brain. After many years of elevated pressure the arteries stiffen in the heart, brain, and kidneys, damaging these organs. The heart grows weaker and unable to pump blood to the rest of the body. Slowly, surely, silently, the body deteriorates.

Daily treatment of hypertension with a medication that reduces blood pressure to normal will stop this abnormally rapid deterioration of vital organs.

The hallmarks of illness caused by malfunction are the following:

1. Loss of normal function of an organ or tissue.
2. Possible presence of the disease in other family members.
3. A course that usually waxes and wanes but persists throughout life.
4. Ability to have improved function but inability to have a complete cure.

### ILLNESS OF DEGENERATION

Most patients can gracefully accept the chance of contracting an infectious illness. Few tolerate the lifelong bother of a malfunction. Only the most saintly consider degenerative problems preludes to heaven. These illnesses of old age often begin in middle age, and are often superimposed upon malfunctions and a life weakened by physical infections, emotional upheavals, and spiritual testings. The worst illnesses for a tired body to bear are the unremitting, progressively downhill processes that eventually end in death.

Many patients do not want to accept the degeneration of later life. They persistently seek for some miracle cure for their ailments. They deny the illness, suppress its pain, and reject the reality of aging. They turn to copper bracelets, special diets, nutritional supplements, antigravity machines, chelation therapy, and a host of other marginal remedies. These patients implore physicians for the best specialty care, the newest laser therapies, or the latest surgical technique.

We are a generation woefully hooked on youthful appearance and energy. We disdain the thought of bodily deterioration and aging. Even many Christians continue to invest heavily in their earthly bodies, forgetting a heavenly savings account that will not rust, tarnish, decay, or die (Matt. 6:20, 21).

Because degenerative disease is the most difficult for patients to comprehend and accept, it becomes the most important for the professional counselor to understand.

Here, too, some examples will help.

Osteoarthritis is usually considered a degenerative disease, though recent research suggests abnormal antibody responses may affect the joint tissues.[12] The fingers become gnarled and stiff. The hips and knees grind with motion and excruciating pain often occurs simultaneously. The neck and back begin to crumble, pushing the elderly patient into a hunchbacked posture.

Modern medicine has devised ways to relieve the discomfort—temporary repair through joint replacement, a slowing down of the process with oral anti-inflammatory agents. But eventually the body succumbs.

Dementias also cause premature degeneration, but they affect the cells of the brain. As these cells are destroyed, brain function slowly deteriorates. In the early course, a dementia impairs short-term memory. Later it progresses to problems with vision, communication, and hearing. The aging adult slowly lapses into a childlike state requiring regular care and help in feeding and dressing. This is the typical course and process in Alzheimer's dementia.[13]

No available treatment cures brain cell deterioration; the best only arrest it temporarily. Some people cling to the hope of dying from another illness before they lose their faculties.

Many of these degenerative diseases have no cures. The few therapies available relieve the pain and retard the destruction. They are called palliative treatments because they cannot cure, only comfort.[14]

The hallmarks of degenerative illness are the following:

1. A beginning in middle or late life with progressively decreasing function.

2. Resistance to improvement through medical therapy, although some comfort and slowing of the process can be obtained.

### INDIVIDUALITY OF AN ILLNESS

Most parents like the simple, cut-and-dried approach to medicine of the family medical encyclopedia. It is usually easy to look up a group of symptoms, find the most appropriate diagnosis, and develop a home remedy for their child's illness— or so it seems.

Both patient and physician like simplified medicine. When treating individuals with individual diseases, however, this is not good medicine. Tailoring treatment to the specific process and symptoms of the patient yields much better results—just as a counseling program must consider the specific psychodynamics of a patient and family.

The unfortunate experiences of the Cook family illustrate the individuality of illness. Early one summer everyone in the family came down with the flu. It started with their seven-year-old. She had a fever of 104 degrees, nausea, vomiting, and sores in her mouth. For three days her illness continued, and she remained unable to hold down fluids. Admitted to the hospital with dehydration and viral meningitis, she was successfully treated with close observation and intravenous fluids.

While the seven-year-old was still in the hospital, both Mom and Dad became ill simultaneously. Mom was fortunate. She just had fever with shaking chills and sore throat. Dad wasn't. He had nausea, aches, runny nose, and a profuse diarrhea that struck every fifteen to twenty minutes for about a day. The stomach cramps were almost overwhelming at times, and once he even passed out from the pain.

About forty-eight hours after Mom became ill, their eleven-month-old baby became irritable. She had a consistent temperature of ninety-seven degrees when checked and the strangest rash they had ever seen: big bumps, little bumps, flat red blotches, and red circles with clear centers covered her from scalp to toes. Most of the time, the baby was happy and active in spite of the rash.

Each family member had different symptoms; and a trip to the medical encyclopedia might have suggested that each had a different illness. Yet the culprit was the same Coxsackie virus in each person. In one case it required the hospital, in another, aspirin; in another, diarrhea medicine; and in the baby, medication for her rash.

The same illness almost never expresses itself identically in two different people. Two individuals may have strep throat; but one may have fever, nausea, and sore throat while the other has rash and sore throat. No two diabetics will be exactly alike. Both will have different needs for insulin, diet, and exercise. Different complications will occur as well. Osteoarthritis will affect the hands of the carpenter, but bother the hips and knees of the mail carrier.

The sooner we can convince our patients that infection, malfunction, or degenerative illness affects each person uniquely, the sooner the patient will put aside emotional reactions and start accepting the illness.

### RECURRENCE OF ILLNESS

Illness and infection will occur throughout life. Malfunctions will wax and wane. Degenerative diseases will continually progress and plateau. These are the natural laws of disease.

Recurring disease is an effective reminder of death's inevitability and the need to be spiritually prepared. This is the spiritual purpose of disease, suffering, pain, and death.

What are the emotional dynamics of recurrent illness? How can it be so devastating cognitively and emotionally? Is it possible to be maturing and then return to the reaction phase when illness recurs?

Without the cognitive and emotional acceptance of illness or spiritual acceptance of eventual death, recurring symptoms can cause utter emotional devastation. Hopes built by initial gains are dashed to pieces. Regained function is lost again. The already fragile, recovering self-esteem falls even lower. The rungs of the social and occupational ladder break beneath the feet. Few things in life are as discouraging as severe, recurrent illness.

Imagine being the woman with the "issue of blood" mentioned in scripture. Imagine the grotesque treatments that were used, the potions, the incantations, the anointing oils, the cathartics. Imagine her ups and downs with the many different physicians she saw. She put up with her illness for eighteen long years, each time having her hopes dashed when treatment failed. Try to understand the psychologic devastation that must have marked her life. With such a low self-esteem, it is amazing that she could muster enough courage to push her way through the crowd to touch the hem of Christ's garment.

Now, imagine her joy at being physically, emotionally, and spiritually healed. All healing in Scripture—healing the demonic, healing the paralytic, and healing this woman—goes beyond physical healing alone—it includes the emotional and spiritual aspects, and the changed lives of those healed demonstrate it.

No situation brings people to their spiritual knees more completely than recurrent physical illness. Either the individual rejects God's purpose for this illness and remains separated from God, or the person recognizes a mortal need for a Savior and accepts his grace.

In either case, those who experience recurrent illness, continuing degeneration, or multiple ailments need tremendous psychological support. Each problem previously discussed will be deeper—the losses greater, the family dysfunction more profound, the acceptance harder, the reassessment more depressing, and the goals more difficult to obtain. The counselor's job will be more difficult, and the close proximity of severe illness or death will place tremendous stress onto the counselor's shoulders.

The task will be immensely easier if the counselor returns to basics. With each recurrence, remind patients of the expected ups and downs of any disease process. Counsel them to work through the emotional reactions and psychological defenses, to understand the course and process of their diseases. Hopefully, this will lead to acceptance and move them into the early stages of growth. We should continue the counseling process into the growth phase, consistently encouraging and exhorting them to new goals and new assessments. It is a ministry of discipling them to grow as the Holy Spirit allows.

The way our patients handle recurrent illness is a good index to their emotional and spiritual maturity. Once individuals understand the course, the waxing and waning, of their illnesses, they can be prepared for a setback. The immature will revert to anger and depression over time. The mature will see this as an opportunity to test resolve and move forward with little or no external motivation. Spiritual maturity will be evident from the individual's ability to study, pray, and share Christ's love with others.

## ENJOYING ILLNESS

God has always used illness to bring men and women closer to himself. There is nothing quite as humbling, no situation that brings our mortality to mind more effectively than physical and emotional disease. And this appears to be what God has intended. We all need restraints to call us back to reliance upon our Father's grace and sufficiency when we stray too far from his loving hand.

I can give instance after instance of friends who came to Christ because of illness, of patients who trusted him on their deathbed, of families saved by the illness of a believing loved one. No more effective time occurs to offer the simple gospel of Christ, and no more likely time for a person to receive him. What an opportunity counselors, pastors, physicians, evangelists, deacons, and believers miss if they do not visit the ill as often as possible to offer the gift of eternal life.

Illness is a time to renew a relationship with the heavenly Father, a time to mature through testing, a time to gain patience through waiting upon him, a time to remember that our weakness, our illness, our thorn in the flesh is the opportunity for his strength to be made perfect in us (2 Cor. 12:7–10).

Life without pain, suffering, and illness would be a continual temptation to live for pleasure alone without fear of retribution. Without pain, we would destroy our bodies, piece by piece, unable to feel when a part is in trouble. Without physical illness, we would consider our bodies invincible, not subject to the curse of death. Without emotional suffering, our desires would be uncontrollable. We would never grow in our relationship with God—in trust, in reliance, in prayer, and in faith.

If God intended illness for our ultimate good, why shouldn't we enjoy God's working in our lives? It will make living with illness much more tolerable.

Does this mean that God wants us to enjoy pain for its own sake? Not at all! God does not want any of us to suffer needlessly. Much of the pain and suffering in our world we inflict upon ourselves. More than 70 percent of all traffic fatalities involve drunk driving. Most lung cancers, heart attacks, and hardening of the arteries are due, in large part, to smoking. The AIDS epidemic is the result of homosexual and heterosexual promiscuity, and intravenous drug use. As many as 95 percent of all premature deaths could have been prevented by simple, "righteous" living.[15]

The Creator knows his design and plan for pain in a person's life. He has also designed ways for it to be more easily tolerated.

It is well-proven that the amount of pain we feel diminishes when we have positive attitudes, hope for the future, and a "merry heart." Scientific studies show increased ability for the immune system to fight infection and to heal illness when hopeful attitudes abound.[16] Studies also show the negative effect of stress, little sleep, and negative emotions. A pioneer in understanding these changes was Hans Selye.[17]

One widely read book about the power of enjoying illness for helping the body heal is Norman Cousins' *Anatomy of an Illness.* Writing from a secular approach, Cousins describes how his positive outlook and motivation helped dramatically in healing severe illness.

I made the joyous discovery that ten minutes of genuine belly laughter had an anesthetic effect and would give me at least two hours of pain-free sleep. When the pain-killing effect of the laughter wore off, we would switch on the motion-picture projector again (to view a humorous movie), and, not infrequently, it would lead to another pain-free sleep interval.[18]

49

Present medical theories suggest that endorphins, morphine-like brain hormones may be secreted during certain "natural highs" such as in stress or running.[19] These, and other self-produced hormones, modulate the pain response, making suffering more tolerable. It is a built-in system, designed by a loving heavenly Father to bring relief and comfort as the victim reaches toward God. As with all of God's beautiful creations, this system can be distorted and its drugs abused to bring self-indulgent pleasure.

Those with nothing to do but think of pain all day long feel it more intensely and deteriorate more quickly. Prisoners of war have found, after being tortured, that getting their mind off the pain as quickly as possible helped. Some recited memorized Scripture, others designed buildings, and some ran elaborate electric train sets in their minds. The more they concentrated on something pleasant and enjoyable, the longer they could endure the torture and loneliness.

This simple concept can be taken one step farther. Those who take their minds off their own problems to help others seem to forget their own problems. Helping others not only brings eternal rewards but may also relieve physical and emotional suffering.

Counseling patients to see the positive side effects of illness, helping them divert their minds from their problems by helping others, keeping a positive, realistic attitude about recovery, and remembering that "a merry heart doeth good like a medicine (Prov. 17:22)" are the tasks that will be most therapeutic. If we, as health professionals, can keep these uplifting concepts in mind as we listen, counsel, and treat our patients, those who are ill will respond more quickly. They will be more apt to accept their situations with God's grace and be filled with more hope of recovery.

# CHAPTER THREE

# HEALTH CARE AND ILLNESS

Many cityscapes display the cold, sterile, but beautiful outlines of new hospital buildings housing the greatest, most advanced technological care offered to man. These for-profit hospitals and their parent corporations further the technological quality of care, spending millions on such research projects as mechanical hearts, bionic limbs, or eyes for the blind. They are the wonder of modern medicine, and they offer investors a large profit.

Yet the halls, the rooms, the operating theaters, and the emergency departments, all convey sterility, coldness, and fear. Designed for convenience and function, these areas feature cold, hard surfaces installed for ease of cleaning. Rooms are designed to fulfill the needs of the physicians, nurses, physical therapists, and x-ray technicians who perform in them.

Unfortunately, our patients' emotional needs have often been excluded from these designs, but they are the very people who need our help to heal. The system is not designed to relieve the turmoil that accompanies an illness. Our patients are fighting for emotional sanity in the midst of suffering, but these complex medical environments do not soothe their fears, their depression, or their tears.

What can the patient and counselor do to counteract the emotional devastation brought on by such a system? It is essential for the counselor who desires to minister to the emotional needs of the ill to understand how medical care is given and in what environment it is received. Once patients cognitively understand the disease process, course, treatment, and prognosis, they can emotionally accept the losses, changes, relationships, and new environment where care will be received.

This chapter will explore the medical settings where sick people live. Just as Christ ministered to people where they live, so we can minister more effectively once we understand the nature and functions of care given and the environments where it is received. Our task will be to humanize a sterile, technological, profit-oriented medical care system, helping our patients accept their trials and mature through them.

### ABSENCE OF CARE

"Doctor, you just have to see me today! This is an emergency, and no other doctors in town will see me because I am on Medicaid."

The forty-year-old woman had demanded to talk with me personally on the phone—or else she would do something drastic to herself.

This patient told a sad story. Her husband was in jail for theft. He was an alcoholic, had problems keeping a job, and needed money for medicine for the children. As the story goes, he was too proud to ask for welfare. In his distress, he had borrowed, swindled, and cheated a number of people out of money. When his wife went to see him in jail, she was told, "Oh, yeah. He hanged himself in his cell. We just found him."

She was left with two teenagers, a huge pile of bills, and deep physical and emotional scars from that relationship. She recounted severe drunken beatings, several incidents of rape, and sexual and emotional assaults upon the elder daughter that had included beatings and burnings.

We agreed to see her as a patient. That afternoon she showed up in the office.

"Doctor, I just can't hold down any food," she said. "My stomach aches all the time. I feel like I got balloons in my belly. I got headaches all the time. I feel weak and just can't take care of the apartment. You just got to help me feel better so I can take care of the kids."

Her physical complaints were almost endless. Every time we discussed one problem, examined that area, and made a plan for securing diagnosis and treatment, she was already well into explaining another problem. It took two hours to give this lady "a little care."

Situations like hers, however, are commonplace in our cities and in many rural areas. Every physician I know has ministered to many such patients. People in our society who are least able to afford health care are often most demanding and most needy.[1] Though she could have been seen in the emergency room, free clinic, or public health department, what my patient really needed was emotional care and counseling. That was absent for her—as it is for many, many others.

Why do so many patients continue to seek physical care for symptoms of emotional distress? Why is our medical care system so insensitive to these emotional needs?

## Sterile Health Care

Problems and inequities within the health care system abound. Two of the most glaring causes are the desire for profit and poor physician-patient communication.

Profits within the medical care system have grown tremendously over the past twenty years, and they now account for 10.9 percent of the gross national product.[2] Everyone is out for his or her share of this. Physicians who have trained for many years have huge debts from medical school. They work extremely long, exhausting hours. It is only natural that they feel an excellent salary is due them for the hardships endured. Hospitals also need sufficient funds to operate. They must charge patients or their insurance companies excessively to offset losses from those who are poor, unable, or unwilling to pay. The insurers are wedged in the middle. They charge employers enough to guarantee a buffer against inflation, pay hospital bills and administrators, and give stockholders a sizable profit every year.[3]

Offices and hospitals are designed to give the best technological care to the most people with the greatest possible profit margin. Caring for patients emotionally takes extra time and money and greatly reduces profit. Many view it as a nonessential expense. Although some hospitals have added people to brighten the physical environment and ensure a human touch, they also charge more for these services to maintain the almighty profit margin.

Is it any wonder that a poor, downtrodden woman with no husband, car, home, job, or cash—and having to take care of two children—is not wanted in our medical system? Such a drain on profit could be better spent on new technology—the same marvelous devices that keep broadening the communication gap between patient and physician.[4]

New technologies can save many lives. They probe deeper, understand more, treat what has been untreatable. But when a technology is unavailable, costs too much, or doesn't help a particular patient, it is difficult to explain adequately to an anxious or dying person. It makes medical care seem unfair, and it widens the communication gap.

Many physicians are unable to communicate the complexities of medical practice or these new technologies to their patients. Patients, on the other hand, hear of these great medical marvels and expect a perfect result every time they are treated. Some patients will not be satisfied with their results, whether or not the physician was at fault, and desire a handsome profit for their discomfort. Lawyers, eyeing profits for themselves, are very willing to help these unsatisfied patients obtain their "deserved" rewards.

A profit-oriented medical system, an extremely complex medical system, a poor-communication medical system is the monster we all must face. It is the system that gives us our health care.

Unfortunately, it is when we are most vulnerable—physically ill, weak, tired, and emotionally distraught—that we enter it.

The need for emotional care calls out for good counselors, counselors who have the expertise to guide their patients through this medical system. Counselors and pastors take on increasing importance as physicians become less and less able to perform the "emotional" healing so crucial to physical recovery.

What are some of the problems within the medical care system, within specific avenues of care? How may counselors bring "emotional healing" to a system that lacks it?

### Care in the Physician's Office

The beginning of our present health care problem is the physician's office. Patients are channeled through the office for convenience, efficiency, and fee collection—for the physician. The patient-physician relationship begins with the ominous, foreboding names of the environment—the "waiting room," the "examination room," and the "billing office." These send subliminal messages to the patient that the physician is in control upon entering the door.

No wonder I have heard the comment—"No offense, but I just can't stand going to doctors"—about a thousand times in my career. Patients' first impressions of the medical system are: convenience for the physician, control over life and limb by the physician, and control over finances by the office staff. This begins the relationship on the wrong foot.

Only a gentle, caring, unhurried physician can bring a sense of humanity and patient control back into this sterile system. If the physician's demeanor is cold and technological, or if too many patients are demanding his time, a trusting relationship will never develop between two people who need to share intimately with one another.[5]

Patients would find a pleasant change if physicians greeted them at the door and welcomed them into the office. What would happen if the staff went out of its way to make sure they were comfortable, their coffee cup filled, their wait as short as possible? It would certainly be a better way to start a trusting, caring relationship.

The patient—to achieve a truly therapeutic relationship with a physician, counselor, psychiatrist, or pastor—must be able to share intimate, sensitive information and trust in the opinion and personality of the caregiver. As in all relationships, trust is built by two-way communication, sharing of ideas and opinions, and a warm emotional response between the participants. Patients often select their primary care physician on a friend's recommendation and continue the relationship if they can establish rapport and trust.[6] The physician must trust patients to give a full and precise history, to offer a truthful recollection of events. It is the patient's responsibility to faithfully complete appropriate therapies and take prescribed medications. In our present legal climate, it is risky for a physician to continue serving a patient who gives false information or refuses therapies. A non-compliant patient should be dismissed from the practice before communication completely breaks down and a lawsuit is filed.

When an office environment is not conducive to building a trusting, caring relationship and a physician is too busy to spend time with the patient, there is little basis for a patient-physician relationship.

The only thing left is expertise.

### Belief in the "Almighty" Physician

The "Father of Western Medicine," as Dr. William Osler was affectionately titled, often wrote about the relationship between physician and patient in the late 1800s. He described the most effective therapies at Johns Hopkins University Hospital as "an atmosphere of optimism, and cheerful nurses. . . ." The physician with the best reputation in the United States, he attributed his healing success to aspects of personality and behavior independent of his scientific knowledge of medicine.[7] A colleague, Dr. William Henry Welch wrote of Osler, "The instant he entered the sick room, the patient felt better. The art of healing seemed to surround his physical body like an aura; it was often not his treatment but his presence that cured."[8]

The same holds true today. A physician's reputation as an authority on some illness and the faith the patient invests in that reputation may be more curative than the therapies prescribed. The amount of trust that exists is directly proportional to the reputation of the physician in the community, among medical colleagues, and in academic stature. A physician's ability to use powerful new technologies and machines can breed an almost worshipful faith from patients.

The major determinant of the physician-patient relationship becomes the physician's specific expertise in diagnosing and treating illness. Since this seems to be the prime reason for trust, the relationship becomes severely lopsided. One member, the physician, holds immense power over the other. The other member, the patient, feels this loss of control and can become passive and non-contributing in the healing process.

Many patients who desire an equal partnership in the healing process have lost respect for the physician or for the care they receive. Their trust has been supplanted by an attitude of tolerance—they endure coming to a physician. Many come only when deathly ill. They come when fear of what the illness will do to themselves, or their children, becomes too great.

Others see this patient-physician relationship as adversarial: "You have what I want, and I am going to get it." These patients are often demanding and stubborn. They desire diagnoses that fit their understanding of the illness. They are also the ones who forget their checkbooks or have financial problems when the time comes to pay the bill. They win when they get better without paying for it, and they rationalize that "the doctor gets paid too much anyway."

Many physicians feel this adversarial relationship and grow increasingly defensive. They order extra tests to cover their costs. They swiftly discharge a patient who complains about service, doesn't pay his or her bill, or refuses to comply with therapies.

Few are the physicians who excel in their practice, effectively teach patients about their illness, and eagerly build a mutual, trusting, caring relationship with a majority of them. Where are the William Oslers, the Paul Brands, the "Marcus Welbys," the caring "country docs" of our society?

## Counselors in the Medical Office

This "high tech-low touch" health care system has bred the need for nonspecialist family physicians to help patients enter the complex world of medicine. It has also dramatically increased the need for trained counselors, social workers, and pastors to restore humanity to medical care. Many group practices of family physicians are overwhelmed by the counseling needs of patients, and so they hire a counselor or social worker to join them. Since technology cannot be set aside, physicians, whether they want to or not, must specialize in the complexities of practice and leave the emotions untreated or referred to a counselor or pastor.

The physician's group practice offers excellent opportunities for counselors or pastors to interact with ill clients. The medical office is a safe, effective place for patients to deal with their emotional reactions to illness, family situations, conflicts, or losses of all types. It is a professional environment where patients can express emotional needs and deal with them without facing the possible stigma of a referral to a psychiatrist's office.

The medical office often refers patients to the hospital for care, allowing the professional counselor to minister in that environment as well.

## THE NEED FOR HOSPITAL CARE

The medical office, with its many emotional quirks, creates a moderate amount of anxiety in most patients. The need for hospitalization magnifies all of the communication problems and relational problems seen in the physician-patient relationship. It also presents a "higher tech-lower touch" environment that can develop into severe anxiety in patients because of a greater void of emotional care.[9]

The hospital environment is more complex than the office. Patients are taken to the admitting office and interrogated about personal and financial information. When they arrive in a room, all clothing is removed, personal effects are taken, and they are introduced to a nurse who is available "when you push the button." Patients live in a noisy, strange, and cold environment, in a bed that is new and uncomfortable, and with people who perform unpleasant tasks—blood tests, injections, and barium enemas. During this unpleasant wait, thoughts about "what the bad news is going to be" fill the mind and frighten even the most courageous.

What can be a frightening, cold, sterile place may be partially humanized when caring people get involved with testing and treatment. The physician can, and should, be the greatest soother. He or she should take sufficient time to discuss the need for hospitalization with patients, to explain various tests and their purposes, to describe the sensations they will experience and the expected outcomes of diagnosis or treatment. Time limitations, however, keep many physicians from spending more than a few minutes with each patient, giving direction as to new testing or treatment. Few physicians spend adequate time to dispel the daily fears and anxieties that rise from the emotional turmoil of illness.

### The Information Collector Role

Counselors, pastors, nurses, family, and friends can provide the necessary emotional support to hasten the emotional healing process. Often a family member will serve as information collector. He or she will track down the physician, ask specific questions about test results, find out why certain treatments are given, and discover what specific symptoms mean. The family messenger then digests this information and gives it to the patient and other family members in more understandable terminology. This information collector, especially when a family member, may also become the chief decision-maker and negotiator in the patient's behalf. During a time of physical and emotional weakness, many patients depend heavily upon family and want all decisions made for them.

Counselors and pastors may be asked to fill this role, offering to collect information, negotiating, and even helping make decisions about treatment options. It may be more comforting for a professional counselor to discuss a patient's health care with the professional physician. Yet from a legal and ethical standpoint, physicians cannot release medical information to a non-family member unless so instructed by the patient. It is wise for the professional counselor to help the patient make proper treatment decisions without ever taking control of the process from patients or family.

Humanizing the process of hospitalization can be accomplished in a number of ways, and for the sake of the patient's

59

emotional health and healing ability, it may be best accomplished by the counselor. Let patients know you are available as needed, and make regular visits to show support. You may want to sit down with them and complete an "emotional support care plan" (see the Appendix). This will include assessing their expectations and fears, setting goals to collect information about their illnesses, identifying other people who can offer emotional support, and allowing them to construct their feelings if a serious or benign diagnosis is discovered. When their feelings and emotional reactions are anticipated and discussed, patients are more likely to accept their illness, promptly reassess their situation, and resolve the emotional conflicts that could slow their physical recovery.

The counselor or pastor should attempt to fit into the routines of the hospital. Visiting hours are the most appropriate time to spend with patients, but other arrangements can be made if family is not present and no other tests are being run. The nursing staff and the patient will appreciate being asked about the most appropriate time to visit. This will often vary from day to day. Being there when the physician plans to talk with the patient or just afterward gives psychological support that may be essential for the tasks of cognitive and emotional acceptance.

Offer to pray with your patients, but be receptive to their desires. It may be better, if they desire solitude, to remind them that you will be praying for their recovery.

Sensitivity and understanding are the two most important counseling qualities for the hospital setting. The patient is already physically weak, tired, and often in pain—and likely to be emotionally drained as well. The patient is in one of the most vulnerable positions he or she can experience. A flippant attitude or conversation can bring further emotional harm. Sensitivity to a patient's words and feelings will bring comfort instead of grief. Assessing how the patient feels, what he or she desires from you, and how to help most should be the object of the visit. The patient had little control when entering the hospital environment, so it is wise to give control back to the person during your caring visit.

In summary, the emotional trauma of the hospitalized patient will be greatly lessened by a caring, sensitive, understanding counselor who helps collect information about the illness and assists the patient in accepting the disease and recovering from it.

## NURSING HOME CARE

As I walked down those sterile, wide, nursing home corridors, I was thinking what it would be like to be caged up in a body I could barely move, waiting patiently for the Lord to call my name.

I was on my way to see my favorite nursing home patient, a dear woman of God who had suffered a recent stroke.

"Sometimes it does feel kind of strange," she explained. "I've often felt like my body was still here, but I was walkin' out the door. But I've found what works. I let the nurses take care of this tired body. Jesus and me are takin' care of my mind."

She spoke up as I was walking back to the nurses' station. "Make sure you bring my love to your wife and children."

Before I was out of hearing range, I could faintly hear the hymn "Victory in Jesus" above the other moans and noises.

The nursing home may represent the greatest loss of control an individual can experience in life. Everything must be cared for: eating, changing position, changing clothing, personal functions, taking medication, walking, moving in a wheelchair—all necessities of care must be handled by a nurse or aide. The patient can feel helpless, angry, dependent, and depressed. If he or she relies solely upon feelings, they become amplified to many times their original size.

In fact, many who are placed in a nursing home for family convenience quickly lose self-esteem, a sense of self-worth, their role, social and family position, their ability to feel—everything except their life. And many desire to lose that as quickly as possible.

Many believe Job may have felt much the same loss of control. Scripture tells of his losses—lands, homes, cattle, children, friends, and health. From a physical perspective, he desired death. Yet after this severe testing, Job's steadfast faith and trust prompted the Lord to restore what he had lost. Job's endurance, resulting from the total loss of control, ingrained in him (and in all saints who have suffered or will suffer severely) the faith to trust and rely upon his God to the point of death (Job 13:15).

The counselor's ministry to patients needing nursing home care, and to their grieving families, is the same as with any new illness: dealing with the losses, giving information about the situation, and helping them accept decreased function. These steps can resolve the conflicts that would hinder physical recovery, emotional comfort, or spiritual maturity.[10] Although many illnesses are degenerative and irreparable, it is amazing the function that can return when emotional issues are settled and the patient is encouraged and rehabilitated.

In Pemberville, Ohio, I once visited a progressive nursing home that bucked the system. Most breed dependence, low self-esteem, and a fatalistic attitude despite trying to protect patients and provide for their care. This progressive nursing home worked hard to improve the patients' expectations about themselves. They helped patients realistically accept their physical limitations, but the staff also pushed patients to exceed their own expectations. They set realistic short-term goals and lofty long-term ones. The nurses, aides, kitchen help, administrators, even family members were recruited to encourage patients to believe in themselves and their capabilities. Depression seldom entered this environment because patients were consistently counseled and encouraged to be positive and to reach or exceed their goals. A large percentage of patients, by nursing home standards (38 to 45 percent), were sufficiently rehabilitated to return to home care. That compares to a rehabilitation rate below 5 percent for the average nursing home.[11]

What is the difference? The patients accepted their illness and their limitations, but they were encouraged to set challenging goals. Positive encouragement, taking their minds away from their misery, working into the *growth* phase with supportive staff and families—these were the most helpful factors in nursing patients out of the nursing home.

How does the counselor help someone endure the losses of nursing home care?

As a runner, I always appreciate yells of encouragement from the crowd, especially when my leg muscles tighten and my chest pulls for every available molecule of oxygen. Those yells and cheers take my mind off the suffering, at least temporarily. They allow me to set some short-term, attainable goals. The more they yell, the more I forget the pain, and the easier it becomes to reach the next goal.

Nursing home patients also need emotional encouragement and mental diversion to help them forget their physical situation. Their minds can stay alert and healthy, and they can have a more positive outlook about themselves. Their families will take encouragement from seeing their loved ones, the ones they have grieved for and suffered guilt over, feeling good about themselves in spite of their limitations.

We can take a lesson from Job's counselors and from this progressive rehabilitation home. We don't need to expound upon patients' problems, their inabilities, their losses, or their sin. We need to be their consistent encourager, always helping them see success in whatever small gains they make.[12] Even when dealing with multiple degenerative conditions, patients' attitudes about their illnesses, their goals, and their successes can move them back home to the families they love.

## HOME CARE

Many people now choose the family home when a family member needs extended hours of care. The prospect of placing the loved one under the care of strangers in a strange environment creates too much emotional stress and shame for the decision-maker to bear. Since most facilities have resigned themselves only to meeting basic physical needs—not physical and emotional rehabilitation—home care becomes a more desirable option.[13] If our patients can stay at home with family help and professional nursing care, why send them to an institution?

The home care option for the elderly or terminally ill has become more accepted because of the equipment available for comfort and care, the increasing number of home care nurses, and the training hospice programs offer dying patients.[14] Insurance and hospital costs are so high that a family's savings can be depleted with one catastrophic illness or with long-term nursing home charges.[15] Furthermore, many insurance plans now pay for equipment and home care for the chronically ill.

There are so many emotional benefits to the home care option. The difficult, distasteful decision to separate the chronically ill member from the family need not be made, and the grieving process is avoided. Separation anxieties, fear of a new environment, and the losses of home, family, and role are avoided, too. When the rest of the family assists an infirmed member, closeness and mutual reliance can result.

But home care can also have some negative aspects. Some people fear having a family member die in their presence or even in their house. They don't believe they could ever use the room again, face other relatives, or have their children see the body. Since they have never witnessed death personally, they fear it as an extremely unpleasant, painful experience.

"What would the neighbors think if I let Father die in my house?" they say.

For some, the nursing home lets the family grieve the loss of their loved one in a slower, more controlled manner. The guilt of abandoning a family member in a nursing home is far less of a problem than the fear of the grieving process.

But, overall, the decision to take care of a family member at home has more scriptural support, depending upon the heart attitude of the decision (Ex. 20:12). Jesus himself argued with the Pharisees about substituting man's tradition for God's commandment to honor and support parents (Matt. 15:1–9).

The decision to seek care from a nursing home should be made *by the patient primarily, in the best interest of the family*. The decision to keep the patient at home should be made *by the family, with the patient's best interests in mind*. Either decision is very difficult. A counselor involved in this process can make sure the emotional and physical needs of each party are met. Assessing needs, not wants, will help families put convenience in proper perspective and give better insight into important aspects of making this decision.

## SELF CARE

A few people with chronic or terminal illness choose to separate themselves from their families. Others have no living relatives. These people may choose self care—home care without the help of family.

Considering the epidemic spread of AIDS, many terminally ill people will not have the support of family or anyone else. These unique and sad situations will tax the counselor, pastor, and physician to the maximum unless an adequate support system is devised through social services, nursing care, hospice, or other social or church programs for the terminally ill.

Someone to visit, to read Scripture, to pray, to talk about current events, to share feelings is the "counselor" most of these patients desire. Dwelling again on gains, not losses; rehabilitation, not symptoms; mental diversions, not self-pity; can encourage and strengthen the lonely self-care patient.

Creative ideas for devising a support system are always possible. The use of pets to keep the patient company, a Sunday school class rotation to bring a gift, adopt-a-grandmother programs, tapes of church services or national programs, reading a book onto tape, fun-giving tasks that can be done from the wheelchair, and a few thousand more ideas can bring cheer, hope, and joy—the three best counselors.

No matter what the medical environment or style of care, our aim as counselors is to recognize the holes and ruts in the road while guiding our patients safely and successfully to a point further along. Understanding the grief process defines the edges of the road. Seeing the acceptance and growth phases as counseling goals will set our sights on the distant highway, our future course. We have discussed some initial potholes that often make for a rough journey—a lack of cognitive understanding of the types, individuality, and outcomes of illness. The technological vehicle that protects us, our medical environment, also has a few quirks and surprises that slow our emotional progress.

Next, we deal more specifically with the emotional reactions to illness, our perceptions of disease, and how to counsel patients to acceptance and maturity.

## PART TWO

# COUNSELING IN TIMES OF SICKNESS

# CHAPTER FOUR

# COUNSELING AND ILLNESS

The typical family practitioner is called upon to treat a wide range of medical illnesses and a myriad of complicated emotional problems that result from them. None is so devastating as a terminally ill young patient. I doubt if I will ever again minister to a patient who illustrates so many counseling needs as Jay, a terminally ill AIDS patient, whom I first met at Miami University.

My fiancée and I were attending the warm-up meetings for a Josh McDowell campaign and were responsible to Jay, one of the Campus Crusade for Christ staff. He struck me as shy and soft-spoken. I loved to hear his thick Tennessee drawl whenever he spoke.

Jay had lived with the pain of his parents' divorce since he was about ten years old. His mother, a beautiful Christian woman, had attempted through her loving, patient behavior to win her husband to the Lord. He consistently refused her love, her sermons, and her religion. Eventually, he moved across town to live with his girlfriend. Jay stayed and was raised by his mother. His father refused to speak to him, never sent cards, never called, never seemed to care if he was alive or dead.

We grew to love him as a brother and co-worker, and we kept in touch over the years as he continued to minister to the students at Miami.

After he left Campus Crusade, he took a job as assistant pastor in a large Baptist church not far from where we lived in Virginia. His responsibilities included the youth and their yearly "Mexican Escapade." In 1979, he had an opportunity to take a group of high school students to Haiti to help construct an educational wing for a church. After much prayer, the group prepared to go.

Jay, two other adults, and twelve high school students made the trip. After adjusting to the climate, they began preparing the cement, the blocks, and the other building materials. Within two days, Jay and three other students became deathly ill, unable to get out of bed. They had profuse vomiting, diarrhea, stomach cramps, and fever. All the remedies they had brought from home seemed worthless, and the symptoms continued for two full days. Only two choices seemed left: either die of diarrhea and dehydration or seek help from a local medical clinic.

The smell of the clinic was almost more than Jay could bear, but he entered with the three other students and got in line. About twenty-five other people were sitting, waiting for medical attention. The screaming of the infants and the filth of the clinic brought new waves of nausea to their stomachs. Finally, their turn arrived and they entered the office.

The room was dark, lit only by a hanging bulb. On the walls were pictures of the skeleton, a medical graph, and a chart showing all the standard acupuncture sites and their effects. Though the physician spoke very little English, it was only seconds and about three questions before he reached for a hypodermic needle and medication and drew up Jay's shot. The lack of sterile technique wasn't nearly as important to Jay or the students as getting back to work as soon as possible. The next day the symptoms had resolved. They returned, in a weakened state, to working in the hot, Haitian sun.

About five years after their trip to Haiti, Jay took another assistant pastoral position in a local church near us. We renewed our relationship, and he started to use our clinic for his medical care. I became his counselor, spiritual encourager, and physician. He was going to need a lot of emotional and spiritual support to help him through the next four, devastating years.

In what couldn't have been worse timing, Jay's sister called him while he was ministering with a youth group in the slums of Philadelphia. She told him to come home immediately—his mother, a victim of metastatic cancer, was not expected to last the night. Jay had spent almost the entire year caring for her needs, and she appeared to be doing well. Now, on his first trip away from her, the worst was just about to happen.

His mother had sustained severe damage from a heart attack and was rapidly showing signs of heart failure. Jay did his best to get there before she died but was a half hour too late. He dealt with shock, grief, and depression for weeks. He was facing not only the death of his caretaker, but also a lifetime of guilt, frustration, discouragement, disappointment, anger, and hatred toward his father. He had given so much care in the last year to the only person who had ever cared for him. That was when he decided to see me, and we started counseling on a regular basis.

Six months after his mother's death, Jay noticed a few bruises that seemed to persist for a long time. He couldn't remember the injuries that caused them. Over the next eight months, he had many bruises for no apparent reason. When he finally came to the office, he had large, tender bruises all over his legs, a few on his back, and a few on his arms. Initial blood studies showed he had almost no platelets—something was destroying them, and his condition had to be stabilized with platelet transfusions.

He was transferred to a hospital in Washington, D.C., for three weeks, released, and then readmitted for surgery a few weeks later. For some reason, the surgery was never performed.

I attempted to find out how Jay was doing, but I could never speak directly with his physician. About three months later,

I ran into Jay at the local food store. He had lost weight and appeared pale but otherwise in good shape. Our conversation seemed polite, although not as warm as before. When I asked about his medical condition, he seemed to skirt the issue—his physicians weren't sure what had caused the low platelet count, "maybe lupus."

I told him to call if he needed medical help or just a listening ear. Two days later, Jay's senior pastor called me.

"I just can't believe what's going on!" he said. "Jay has just not been himself since he got out of the hospital. He's so distant. He seems to get confused when I give him simple instructions. He's made some of the parents angry with him, and he refuses to talk with me about it."

The pastor said Jay had told one group of teens to fast and pray for him because he had a malignant brain tumor. He then told the sixth graders he had a rare form of lupus that was fatal in six to twelve months. "He told us that he was receiving special shots from you every week," the pastor continued. "But twice I called your office to ask Jay to run an errand on the way back to church. He wasn't in your office either time or even scheduled to be there. I just don't understand."

I could tell the pastor was terribly distraught.

It took about three calls to Jay's physician in Washington, D.C., to find the medical information I desperately didn't want to hear. Then I called Jay and told him we had to talk over coffee.

"I just couldn't tell you," Jay said. "I thought if you knew I had AIDS, you would never see me or take care of me again."

I tried to be reassuring as he continued. "But you just don't understand what it's like! If people knew, they would think I was a homosexual or something. I can't understand why God is allowing this to happen—and all from a stupid needle as I was ministering for him." Even though they explained it to Jay repeatedly, he couldn't understand what was happening in his body.

"I've been invaded by some monster," Jay said. "It makes me feel so unclean."

"It's obvious you have a lot to deal with physically, Jay," I said. "And you have a lot of issues to deal with emotionally and spiritually as well. It's going to be a long process and I hope you'll let me help you."

As I finished my sentence, Jay's face lit up. "I'm glad someone else knows. That really helps."

## PERCEPTIONS OF ILLNESS

Edmond Holt Babbit has written:

Sickness and suffering teach us many lessons. They bring new insights, sharpen perceptions, give a new scale of values, aid perspective, shake a person out of complacency, cause him to appreciate life's simple gifts, widen the horizon of knowledge of human experience, and bring into bold relief life's essentials.[1]

We have all seen this statement personified. Illness can be a life-changing, earth-shaking experience, and it can be a negative or a positive experience. It often is both. Our emotional reactions to illness, just as to any loss, depend upon our perception of the cause, course, and purpose.

"Am I going to be in a lot of pain?" Jay asked. "How long will it last? Are there other types of treatments besides medication? Can I work? What will my family think of me? What am I going to do?"

These were a few of Jay's many questions about his illness, and they are all applicable to any illness.

Jay's perception of disease had changed radically as he observed the uncomfortable, life-threatening cancer his mother had endured. No one in Jay's family had ever faced a serious illness before. Influenza, colds, and one bout of pneumonia had been the most serious things he, his sister, or his mother had faced. The difficult up-and-down course, the pain of the chemotherapy treatments, the bone metastasis, the injections—all entered Jay's memory, shaping and reforming his understanding of suffering. He was with her for much of her illness, but absent during her death. She needed him there, and he needed to be there.

Yet the experience of watching helplessly, as his mother suffered, recalled past emotional problems within Jay's family. The guilt associated with his father's leaving, the anger from his father's comments, the empathetic pain when his mother hurt so terribly—all of this turmoil revived and had to be confronted.

73

This same emotional reexamination is a horrible, but common, part of any serious illness.

Dealing with a patient's emotional suffering is complicated. The issues that surface include doubts, fears, blaming one's self for the present illness, and reexamination of the previous emotional traumas of guilt, loss, anger, and bitterness. The counselor should give the patient insight into this process, separate the acute from the chronic traumas, and work to resolve as many of the acute complications as possible. This will move the individual toward acceptance and promote future healing.

I can't think of a better example, nor a better outcome than Jay's. At first he was torn between extreme anger toward his father and the recurrence of a strong grief process for his mother. He had displaced his own fears of dying, of pain and suffering, onto his deep emotional past. Through the counseling process, we began to deal with his own fears, gaining insight that these other issues were just an emotional smoke screen to protect himself from having to deal with the realities of his own sickness. Spiritually, he had no reason for anger because he had forgiven his father. He had no reason for replaying the grief process because his mother was in the presence of the Lord. Once he realized the proper place for these previous traumas, he was able to tackle the real task at hand.

Within a very short time, he had changed "I hate what my father did to my mother" to "I don't understand why the Lord is allowing me to go through this, but I know it will work together for good." He had measured his losses. He had resolved the emotional turmoil over his illness, accepted it, and launched into the emotional growth phase. He gained new spiritual insight that God could use this "unclean" disease and use Jay.

"I now know why the Lord took my mother when he did," Jay later commented. "I don't think she would have been able to emotionally or spiritually understand that her son was going to die of AIDS."

## Perceptions and the Reaction Phase

Physical illness represents a concrete entity, a starting point for a host of emotional changes. As we have seen, each patient's psychological reactions to illness depend on a number of cognitive and emotional issues that shape perceptions of sickness. A cognitive, specific understanding of a given disease and its effects will help the patient dispel fears of the unknown. He or she will have little need for repression, suppression, or denial. Unresolved grief occurs when the patient does not understand these factors. Acceptance and growth do not come until the patient has answered his or her questions about the illness.

A key task for the counselor is to help patients understand the disease in their own terms. Is this disease a spiritual retribution for sin? Is it because of stress from a poor marital relationship? What factors do the patients think could be responsible for making the disease worse—spiritual, emotional, physical, or otherwise?

When we first assess a grieving patient, we must thoroughly understand these patient perceptions of the cause of his illness. Remember to include the physical factors and any present or persistent emotional traumas or conflicts. Discover whether the patient believes that a spiritual cause is present. We should try to assess all complicating psychological factors as well—such as their present support system, persistent dependency needs, and previous psychiatric or psychological illness. The counselor should also find out how these needs were treated.

Using the "Emotional Reactions to Illness" (Appendix) as a framework for counseling will help the ill person begin to identify and assess feelings and attitudes about the cause of illness.

In Jay's situation, a host of previous psychological traumas and persistent unresolved needs influenced the emotional reaction phase of his illness. While working through the denial without counseling, anger became his major stumbling block in dealing with his disease. He was unable to grieve for himself because of the anger he focused on his father. His rage and anger persisted long into the counseling process. It caused episodes of hyperventilation. He would wake from a deep sleep, dreaming of doing harm to his father. Chest tightness, stomach pain, headaches, tiredness, and depressed emotions also persisted until Jay was able to forgive his father. Only then could he start the process of accepting his own illness.

Another psychological need that persisted in Jay was dependency. His guilt over not being present for his mother's death was very difficult for him to resolve. He believed that she had needed him. In fact, he really needed her—especially now that he was sick. Once Jay understood his strong dependence upon his mother, he was able to see God's working in her death. He was also able to transfer some of those needs to a renewed relationship with his father.

The most difficult aspect of Jay's perception of his disease was his unrelenting feeling that God was judging him for sin. The long years of anger, guilt, bitterness, and betrayal that he felt toward his father were rationalized as sin—the sin that God was judging with AIDS. Sin was the cause of so many others contracting AIDS, through homosexual acts or through addiction to drugs. It must have been the cause of his as well.

It took months of counseling to work through this one issue. Repeated explanations of the physical cause of AIDS, how he had contracted the disease, the strange questions from his doctors, a small Florida town's much publicized rejection of three hemophiliac brothers who had AIDS—all had to be explained over and over again. He believed, as many Christians do, that disease is a judgment of God for personal sin.

> They seem to perceive God as the One responsible for bringing them to this point of crisis or death, and they are inclined both to justify themselves and to register their complaint at the harsh treatment they have received. Mingled with this is often the powerful idea that what they are enduring is some kind of punishment inflicted upon them by God.[2]

God becomes the simple and singular cause for disease.

When we look at this spiritual issue from a scriptural perspective, most people miss an essential point—the cause of disease is not as important as its spiritual outcome.

Does personal sin lead to a disease judgment from God? Scripture makes it clear that one purpose of these testings is spiritual growth and maturity. We also see that disease is both a result of the sin nature of man and a retribution for personal sin. God warned the Israelites that disobedience would result in contracting the diseases of the Egyptians (Ex. 15:26). In another example, however, Christ indicated that one man's blindness was not the result of personal sin, but rather "that the Glory of God might be made manifest" (John 9:3). Disobedience to God's commandments has led to plagues and death (Ex. 7:4, Lev. 16). Even the lying hearts of Ananias and Sapphira caused their death (Acts 5:1). There is no one, clear spiritual cause for sickness and death when looking at these examples. Instead many causes emerge.

But Scripture consistently supports one view for the *purpose* of disease, that of turning people from sin and disobedience, and bringing them closer to God. If we allow our patients to dwell on the spiritual causes for disease instead of the spiritual result, they will remain confused, angry, and unable to move toward acceptance. Once we resolve the spiritual result issue and the patient sees purpose, growth, and maturity from the illness, then acceptance becomes much more likely. The patient can accept the disease despite unresolved emotional problems or confusion about physical aspects of the process.

It took some time, but Jay now sees the ultimate result of his disease as spiritually important. Once this became clear, he cognitively understood the physical origin of AIDS, its course, its treatment, and its often fatal outcome. He now accepts his condition and is willing to take responsibility for his future. It has increased his faith that God knows exactly what is best for him.

"I know that he is going to use me in some AIDS ministry to bring many homosexuals, drug abusers, hemophiliacs, and others to the Savior," Jay told me.

## COUNSELING TOWARD ACCEPTANCE

Hilda was as bright, as loving, as capable a seventy-eight-year-old woman as you would ever want to see. The only problem was her body couldn't keep up with her desire to serve and to minister. Her long years of ministry, her years of singing with evangelists and radio broadcasters, her celibate life of service to Christ—all were exemplary. Yet her body was riddled with congestive heart failure, venous insufficiency, osteoporotic bone disease, cataracts, and a few other severe degenerative processes. When I met her she was just days out of the hospital after treatment for the fluid in her legs. She could barely walk, but that didn't matter. As long as she could get from her house to the car, she could get from the car to her seat in the church sanctuary.

Her health was unimportant except that it hindered her. She would apologize for her infirmities as if she could control the degeneration of her aging body. But she was truly sorry that she, at times, wasn't able to serve with her presence in the front row. She never complained about her health, or made an excuse when she did not attend church.

"My hope has never been in this world or in this body," Hilda said. "My hope remains in the Lord who loves me enough to train me for His Kingdom. I can't complain because I'm already getting His best for me." Hilda had accepted the fact that her body was riddled with many degenerative disease processes. She realized living in a sin-filled race meant disease was an inevitable part of the growth of a Christian. Who or what was responsible for her illness was not an issue. She took full responsibility for her diseases and their treatments. She did not have any serious emotional traumas that were not already resolved. She relied completely upon God to meet her needs, and she was not overly dependent on family, on friends, or on her church.

But these are common and important counseling issues to understand. Acceptance of an illness is difficult when your dependence is upon the wrong person, when you refuse to take responsibility for your disease, or when you believe disease only affects other people. In counseling patients toward acceptance of disease, it is important that we understand these issues and how they delay the process.

## Dependency

Illness breeds a dependence that looks for a hand to hold, someone to share the blame, someone to ease the pain and suffering. Dependence upon others and upon the health-care system can make helplessness a habitual behavior. Helplessness destroys hope for the future, for happiness, for normal relationships. Hopelessness leads to a feeling of resignation to circumstances controlling our lives and makes acceptance even more difficult.

Dependence upon people, family members, church friends, and even counselors will lead to a vicious cycle of emotional resignation. Helplessness becomes hopelessness, which in turn leads to self-pity, low self-esteem, and probably depression. This psychological coal chute leads to the dingy basement of our *most base* personality and character traits. The demanding, belligerent, manipulative nursing home patient, for example, makes this depressing slide because of total loss of control.

Part of our shift in dependency lies in the natural process of regression that occurs when otherwise mature, independent adults become ill. They revert to childlike behaviors, becoming dependent upon family and health care staff because of decreased self-esteem, overwhelming fears, irretrievable losses, and loss of control. As patients become more dependent, they should grow in trust toward a loving Heavenly Father. Scripture tells us to come to the Savior as dependent, needy, humble people, relying upon him in childlike faith (Luke 8:16–17).

Our dependence either moves us toward accepting our illness or becoming resigned to it. Dependence on self or worldly supports causes helplessness, lost hope, utter resignation, primal anger, bitterness, and even hatred of ourselves and God. Properly placed dependence upon God, however, builds faith through testings, perseverance, character, maturity, and peace (Rom. 5:4).

## Inevitability

One of my favorite pastors likes to quip about the inevitability of problems:

"You are either just getting over your present problem, are at the beginning of another problem, or will get the phone call tomorrow!"

Death and sickness entered the world through Adam's disobedience to God's command. It resulted in our banishment from the Garden of Eden and our separation from the Tree of Life, which will give continual healing to our heavenly bodies. Death and sickness are ours because of our lineage. But God also warned the Israelites that continued disobedience to the laws of God would increase their diseases and self-destruction:

If you listen carefully to the voice of the Lord your God and do what is right in his eyes, if you pay attention to his commands and keep all his decrees, I will not bring on you any of the diseases I brought on the Egyptians, for I am the Lord who heals you. (Ex. 15:26)

It is a normal defense mechanism to deny deleterious changes in health, kicking against the goad of inevitable illness. But it is not normal to continue to kick with so much force that it damages one's psychological foot. When such strong psychological defenses occur, counselors find them manifested in many unique, creative ways. An elderly gentleman may admit that ninety-eight percent of people who contract lung cancer die from it, but say, "I just know that I am going to make it." The middle-aged man who sustains a heart attack rationalizes that he will be back to work "in two weeks." A young mother being treated for ovarian cancer may suppress her impending future sterility by telling friends she can have another child within two years. These comments all ring of denial, and the common theme throughout is, "Disease happens to others, not me!"

Scripture and reality are very clear—illness and death are inevitable. Displacement of this fact gives temporary comfort until the patient understands that he or she is included in the term "everyone." Directive counseling to reaffirm that illness afflicts everyone, including the patient, will prevent negative emotional responses and draw the patient closer to the therapeutic emotional condition of acceptance. Patients must be helped to accept the realities and responsibilities of their illnesses.

## Responsibility

Someone has attempted to estimate the amount of disease caused by lifestyle problems, addictions, and poor health habits. About 50 to 70 percent of all hospital days, 95 percent of all premature deaths, and a majority of lost workdays can be directly or indirectly attributed to such public health problems as smoking, drinking, drug addiction, venereal diseases, lack of exercise, food addiction, and poor hygiene.[3] This means that if everyone took responsibility to improve his or her lifestyle about half of all disease would vanish. People would still get sick and die, but it would occur later, and they would live happier, healthier lives until then.

People shun responsibility for disease in a variety of ways. Patients often refuse to take responsibility for their part in causing the disease. A smoker with lung cancer may refuse to quit despite the proven fact that stopping would reduce the risk of recurrence and infection. Other patients, however, believe they are responsible for their problems when no causative effect has been shown. An example is the woman with breast cancer who is consumed with finding and eliminating habits she believes are responsible for the cancer. Still other patients place responsibility on an inappropriate source. An alcoholic, for example, may attribute his continued drinking to a nagging wife, although her behavior may actually be the opposite.

Taking appropriate responsibility for previous actions is necessary before patients forsake guilt and forgive themselves for unhealthy behavior. Here are three principles to share with patients during the counseling process:

1. Take responsibility for handling the disease process, whether you are the cause or not.
2. Forgive yourself and others who may have complicated the illness with their actions or behaviors.
3. Take responsibility for the future—your relationship with God, your relationship with your family, and your treatment and recovery from the disease.

## Past Emotional Situations

As patients regress and become more dependent, they often rehearse previous emotional problems and attempt to link them to their present illness. The patient may attempt to shift blame to malfunctioning family relationships. Although these rarely cause physical illness, many psychiatric disorders are precipitated or complicated by dysfunctional relationships. These guilts, angers, and frustrations can lead to major emotional complications that worsen an illness and upset the healing process.

Allowing the patient to rehearse previous traumas is normal and healthy, to a point. The young man who attributes his leukemia to negative feelings toward his abusing, but now deceased, father is dealing with this unresolved guilt. He is displacing the cause of illness onto this past emotional trauma. The counselor can help deal with this unresolved guilt, but the patient must first separate fact from emotional fiction. It is wise to deal first with the inevitability of disease and place causative responsibility upon the malfunctioning blood system and not on the unresolved guilt. The guilt and the lack of forgiveness become more manageable when separated from the illness and dealt with accordingly.

A serious medical situation may demand that past unresolved situations be put aside until the patient has the emotional integrity and strength to deal with them. In such a case, the counselor can spend time listening to the past emotional traumas. Before they become the major issue, however, the counselor should suggest putting them aside, dealing with present situations, and addressing past problems later.

## HEALING THE BROKEN
### PATIENT-PHYSICIAN RELATIONSHIP

A physician is frequently blamed for a patient's ailing health. Statements such as these are common:

> If the physician had performed the surgery correctly my back pain would be all gone.
>
> I've been to three different doctors and each of them has made my stomach problem worse.
>
> Those pills changed my chemistry so badly that I have never gotten back to good health.

Counselors may be called upon to deal with a life-threatening medical situation that develops because of miscommunication or misunderstanding. A broken patient-physician relationship can present a serious danger when a patient refuses to seek attention for a life-threatening illness because he or she mistrusts the physician. A patient may not take medications because of spite, misuse them because of pride, or refuse treatment or surgery because of a stubborn wish to contradict his or her physician. Here the counselor's objective view and communications skills should be used to guide the patient back to the physician or to another competent practitioner.

Admittedly, physicians make mistakes, medications cause side effects, and surgery may make the patient worse. But most of these "physician-made-me-worse" situations are a combination of poor communication, a bad result, or patient irresponsibility. Not all medications work for everyone. Not all surgeries completely cure a given problem. Not all medical advice proves beneficial. This is due both to patient individuality and to numerous complicating physiological and psychological factors.

Physicians are notoriously poor communicators. Even when they try hard, they often cannot find the words to explain extremely complex processes, medications, treatments, and surgeries to their patients. Even if the physician does explain well, the patient still may not understand.

A thirty-five-year-old construction worker had his third lumbar disk surgery four months ago. Each physician tried to explain that the construction worker faced a significant chance of being worse after surgery. Each surgeon did a masterful job in dissecting the protruding disk and repairing the defect. But each time the worker seemed only to worsen.

So how does the patient explain his situation? "Each of these surgeons was a quack. If I had only gone to a chiropractor to start with, I would be better now."

The real explanation for his getting worse could be either a simple physical matter or a complex psychological one. The body replaces damaged tissue with scar tissue. This tissue sometimes impinges on the same nerves the disk was pinching—a plausible physical explanation. The desire to remain disabled, to receive compensation without working, or any of hundreds of possible emotional factors may be changing this patient's pain threshold—a plausible psychological explanation. Although objective, scientific methods can prove when physical factors are not at fault (despite persistent subjective pain symptoms), the patient may still blame the physician.

The counselor can play a vital role in restoring stability to this damaged relationship by being an objective observer. Since most of these "physician-made-me-worse" situations are not the fault of the physician, the counselor can help to transfer this displaced anger back to the process of illness, the inevitability of illness, and the need for personal responsibility. Using patients' own job responsibilities as a model can help them understand this cause-and-effect issue.

For example, suppose this same construction worker builds a house. Six months later the owners sue him because the ceiling sags, the bathtub leaks, and the basement wall has cracks. Is the worker responsible?

The sagging ceiling was the result of two factors. The new owners had moved a two-ton safe up to the bedroom and placed it next to a water bed. Due to the very wet environment, the joists became waterlogged. The owners and the environment are to blame.

The bathtub leaks because of a defect in the tub and because the sub-contracted plumber didn't plumb the drain correctly. This also dripped water into the sagging ceiling.

The basement wall cracked because excessive rain that year overloaded the drains around the foundation. The cause is the weather.

Now the construction worker can identify with the many complex, diverse factors that are also present in the healing profession. He is much more likely to turn his anger away from the physicians, even though he may still cling to his disability pain. But the counselor has made progress toward the final goals of acceptance and resolution.

## Communicating Empathy

In some situations, the counselor will be the "scapegoat" for the patient who subconsciously desires to stay sick. Those counselors who are consulted and who become part of the health-care team are also at risk. This is especially true if the counselor takes on the more directive approach physicians and nurses commonly use—that of directive therapeutic patient control.

To help prevent this displacement of anger to the counselor, he or she needs to maintain a different set of ministering qualities, qualities that set one apart from the rest of the health-care team. Two qualities are especially important—having the time to listen, and showing caring compassion and understanding—often labeled as empathy.

Physicians, nurses, and therapists never seem to have time to listen to the patient's feelings and concerns. They are often viewed as cold and uncaring because of their busyness. Spending time when patients want to talk about their feelings is the most important way to communicate empathy to them. The willingness to listen may be more therapeutic than any medical treatment. The gentle touch of a hand, the concerned expression, the relaxed posture all communicate a feeling of empathy. But avoid cliché phrases, such as "Oh, I understand," when you obviously have not had the surgery or illness in question.

As in all professional situations, communication and relationship-building are the keys to success. Arrange your schedule to be available for ill patients. Take time to listen. Develop the skills to communicate empathy. It will be a great benefit to the patient and to the whole health-care team.

## COUNSELING TOWARD MATURITY

Suppose that a milestone has been reached: your professional skill, your "caring ear," and the patient's insight have brought acceptance of the process of illness. God's sovereignty in the midst of testing has been approved. The patient now assumes responsibility for the disease and the healing process. The physical benefits of reaching this psychological plateau have begun. How does the counselor sustain this positive movement? What does it take to motivate through setbacks to ensure progress? When are the psychological effects of the disease finally resolved?

One model for understanding the roles of patient and counselor during the healing process is to place the patient in the "new convert" role and the counselor in the "pastor" role. Accepting disease is somewhat analogous to accepting Christ as Savior. We accept our sin as our responsibility, understand our need for spiritual healing, and put our faith in God's plan and purpose. Similarly, the patient needs to accept the disease, his or her need for physical and emotional healing, and God's plan and purpose for the illness.

A new spiritual convert has needs identical to those of the

COUNSELING THE SICK AND TERMINALLY ILL

healing patient. The process involves reassessing abilities, needs, desires, and relationships. An innate desire exists to grow, to progress from a childlike, dependent state to a more mature, independent state. Along the way, people require the fellowship of others and wise spiritual and emotional counsel.

## Personal Responsibility and Maturity

When patients accept their illnesses, they have actually resolved a number of emotional issues. Now they can progress to the fullest possible healing. They have resolved their guilt ("was I responsible?"), their anger ("this is unfair"), their denial ("this can't be happening to me"), their fears ("what is going to take place"), and many other areas. Overall, they are willing to take personal responsibility for these areas and ready to enter the growth phase.

Just as the pastor teaches, preaches, counsels, and listens to help the flock mature, the counselor acts in parallel ways toward the healing patient. Feeding the infirmed person spiritual food, allowing expression of emotions, motivating through directive goal-setting, and encouraging "pep-talks" will all help the patient keep on progressing.

Why are some pastors so able to counsel the sick, the grieving, and the terminally ill? Because the most effective skills are the same whether one is pastoring a church or counseling the sick.

It is the patient's ultimate responsibility to improve. Pastors cannot make their people grow, nor can physicians make patients take medication. Instead, the healing patient is wholly responsible for the course and improvement of an illness. Fostering this desire to heal, motivating with new insights, helping set new goals, and maintaining accountability are ways a counselor can encourage the healing process while stressing patient responsibility.

Be wary of the trap of non-therapeutic dependence—patient on counselor, convert on pastor. If the counselor feels the patient cannot heal alone, then he or she should change the relationship. Become a more directive teacher and motivator while underlining the concept of patient responsibility. Non-therapeutic dependence upon the health-care system costs millions of dollars in lost work, disability payments, and unnecessary use of physicians, hospitals, and counselors.

## Progress and Setbacks

Disease states exhibit progress, plateaus, and setbacks. These are normal for both the physical and psychological courses of any illness and should be anticipated.

It is often difficult for a patient to be objective about his or her own situation. An objective counselor can play a large role in helping the patient see small increments of improvement and deriving motivation from them. Help the patient set up rehabilitation goals, short-term and long-term. Use graphs or charts to record progress. Hold the patient accountable for keeping records and completing prescribed treatments. When patients see the positive effect personal responsibility has on improvement, they often generate more motivation.

Minor and major setbacks—and to a lesser extent, progress and plateaus—are to be expected. They do not mean that the patient has to start the growth cycle again. Setbacks are a normal part of degenerating and malfunctioning diseases and can also occur in an infectious process when immune reserves are depleted. To minimize any lost ground, accept setbacks rapidly when they occur and reassess the present situation and future goals.

Psychological setbacks, independent of physical changes, can have an equally damaging effect on rehabilitation. Recurrences of the resolved guilts, fears, and angers foster doubts that a full recovery will ever occur. Other complicating familial relationships may kill progress. Anticipating both physical and psychological setbacks prevents the patient from having to go through the reassessment and acceptance phases time and time again.

## Final Emotional Resolution

No complete resolution of physical illness can happen until we reach our final spiritual maturity in the glorious presence of our Savior. But when does the counselor finish the relationship initiated by illness?

The physical and emotional recovery phase is not complete until symptoms of the disease have gone. This recovery phase replenishes physical strength, immune reserves, and emotional stability so that the patient can withstand further illness. The replenishment time varies from person to person, illness to illness, and with various complicating physical and emotional factors.

Carol had just received an excellent medical report from her physician. There were no signs of the leukemia three full years after her initial diagnosis. She was one of the few and fortunate—no relapses, few side effects, no loss of hair.

Over the past two years, she had resumed a normal lifestyle. Activities at church included nursery work, the ladies' fellowship, and occasional opportunities to sing or play the piano at other churches. Her full-time occupation was caring for two of the most energetic boys that ever blessed a family. And she was an excellent mother.

After hearing the great medical report, Carol's husband decided to surprise her with a gift. It was a mink coat like her grandmother's, the one she had always wanted.

Her reaction shocked everyone—Carol, her husband, and her counselor. She cried for hours after she saw her gift.

"I am not sure that I understand, Carol. Why was a mink coat so upsetting to you?" her counselor asked.

"When I looked at the coat, I just thought 'I've wanted one for such a long time,'" she sobbed. "My husband told me as he gave me the coat, 'I hope you enjoy it for a very long time.' That started my thinking. How long do I really have? Will someone else be wearing 'my' mink coat? I just couldn't stop crying after thinking that someone else was going to be wearing that coat."

Carol's husband meant to cheer and encourage her after such a good checkup. But in her emotionally weakened state, the gift was understood in ways that were not intended. She had been through such a physical and emotional ordeal that she was bound to crumble when her doubts resurfaced. She had not yet finished her emotional recovery.

Emotional resolution has occurred when patients can voice acceptance of the disease process, resolution of fear, and apathy toward a cause—"It doesn't matter how it happened or who caused it, I know I am through the storm." Once patients have accepted their situation, dispelled their fears of further problems, and resolved the issue of cause, then they are unlikely to need further counseling to help with the issues of this illness. This is where the secular counselor considers patients sufficiently well to be dismissed.

At this time, patients are just entering the growth and maturation phases of their illness. Gaining spiritual insights, developing a deeper faith, and growing toward the image of Christ are some of the goals counselors should set for the rehabilitation and growth phase of an illness. As this maturation becomes visible in the life of the patients—and appears to be self-generated—then it is time to step aside and let them continue on their own.

The one notable exception to this rule is the supposed resolution of a chronic illness that has been complicated by addiction. The addicted individual will always need encouragement, motivation, and psychological support just to maintain sobriety. Unfortunately, these individuals prematurely wrench themselves from therapy because of addictive desires and an overworking denial mechanism.

Jay is a quite different individual today. Initially, he thought he was going to "beat this AIDS thing." All he had to do was eat right, sleep eight hours a night, take vitamins, read his Bible, and God would take the suffering and possibility of death away. Such was not the case.

About four months ago, Jay was admitted to the hospital with double pneumonia. Not just the ordinary bacterial type that could be cured with antibiotics, but the bizarre type called *pneumocystis carinii* pneumonia that AIDS victims get. He could barely breathe. He felt like he was drowning in his own secretions. It was days before experimental drugs started to take effect. It seemed like lifetimes. But it took this much illness to make Jay realize, "I can't trust in doctors, hospitals, or medications. I can only trust in God to pull me through if that is his will."

The treatments changed. Jay was started on AZT to help prevent the deterioration of the disease. He was on weekly injections to help prevent the pneumonia.

But Jay wasn't trusting in the treatments.

"I know I am an innocent victim of AIDS," he said. "But like Joseph, what the world sees as wickedness and evil, God can use in my life to produce spiritual fruit in others dying of AIDS. I can truly say that I am glad that I have AIDS because I know that God is going to use it for good."

# CHAPTER FIVE

## COUNSELING THE ACUTELY AND CRITICALLY ILL

The first time David's mother approached the intensive care unit disbelief and grief so overwhelmed her that she slumped to the floor in tears. After mustering the strength to get up, she entered the dimly lit room to hear the breathing machine pushing and relaxing every five seconds to pump air into David's body. The other pestering sounds—the beeps, buzzers, and blips—all sounded like insects diving after a meal. Odors seemed to emanate from the machines, and the room had a nauseating, pungent smell—as if washed in a concoction of soaps and cleaning fluids.

But all she could see were the tubes, the intravenous lines, the tape, the monitor patches, and the catheters that seemed to engulf David's clean, mostly uncovered body like a nest of serpents. A sheet covered him from the thighs to the navel. His few bruises and scrapes were clean and well tended.

Why wouldn't he move? How could this be happening? How could a little bump on the head have put him in this condition? His mother slumped to the floor with hysterical tears, shouting "It can't be! It can't be! It can't be!"

David had always been a good Christian boy. He was never any trouble. Police found no traces of drugs or alcohol in the car he had been driving when he lost control. The state patrol estimated his speed at ten mph over the speed limit and believed that the sharpness of the curve, the slight increase in speed, and a problem in the steering mechanism all contributed to the accident. Both he and his girlfriend were thrown from the car—she walked away with cuts and bruises, while he lay dying in the Intensive Care Unit.

The family had lost its father ten years earlier to a plane accident—now they had to deal with the real possibility of losing the "baby" of the family as well. What an emotional struggle occurred over the next five agonizing days about whether to keep him on total life-support or to pull the plug. Their hospital vigil was day and night, always talking with David, praying with him, encouraging him, loving him. They never ceased to believe God could pull David through when the physicians repeatedly said he was brain dead.

God and David made the final decision. On the fifth day, David's vital signs began to drop. Within thirty minutes, even the machines could not keep him alive. He never regained consciousness.

The next case has a happier ending, but the reader should be forewarned that this case contains graphic detail. If the counselor or pastor cannot emotionally handle being in the presence of a shattered body, such as is described in this case, he or she should take care before visiting an Intensive Care Unit. A quiet room should always be provided for the counselor and family to spend time together.

Of the four young men in this accident, Stephen was the most seriously injured. This group of Bible college students had been traveling from church to church, in the eastern states, preaching, singing, and teaching. While traversing an interstate highway late at night, a light rain began to freeze on the roads. An eighteen-wheeler was in the process of passing their van when the truck lost control, jackknifed across the road and crushed the van as it slid.

Stephen's family was rushed to the next state where the accident occurred. Even as they entered the surgical intensive care unit, the physicians stopped them and asked if they could use some of Stephen's organs for transplant—he was only minutes away from death.

"We have to ask Jesus whether he is going to live or die first," his mother said.

As they entered the room, the reality of death came over them. The view of his smashed body told them how serious the situation was. Both legs were broken in many places, and a number of large lacerations and bone fragments protruded. His legs and hips all seemed out of joint, broken from the impact. His chest appeared crushed on one side, with scrapes and bruises all over. Beyond the breathing tube, the intravenous lines, the monitor cables, the chest tube, the Foley catheter, the slings and sand bags they could see that the top of Stephen's head was opened. The skull and the brain were exposed. His face was so swollen that he probably could not have opened his eyes or mouth had he tried.

The physicians repeatedly came to the family and asked for the use of his organs. Each time the family would retreat to the prayer chapel to employ the only offensive weapon Stephen had—the power of prayer.

After fourteen days of total unconsciousness, he began to respond. The physicians now had reason to fix the skull fractures, the shattered legs and hip, and the crushed chest. Over the next six months, he recovered sufficiently to communicate basic needs. He could even take a few steps. Many months of physical and emotional rehabilitation—and the hope of being able to preach again—kept Stephen and his family praying and working for a complete recovery.

Recently, ten full years after the accident, Stephen stepped into a pulpit, preached a miracle message about a miracle God and saw three people turn to Christ. Only the prayers of God's servants, the love, devotion, and trust of the family, and the miraculous power of God could have done such a great work.

## THE ACUTE HEALTH CRISIS

Fortunately, most people do not personally experience the pain and suffering of a major auto accident and the need it brings for intensive health care. But all experience serious health crises directly or through a beloved family member. As shown in Table 1, most deaths in the United States are caused by acute health situations.

Acute health crises—like a father dying of a heart attack, a young mother bleeding to death from a delivery, a child being kept alive by machines after taking poison—all result in devastating psychological changes to the patient and loved ones. Patients and families display a range of psychological responses which effective counseling strategies must consider.

### Psychological Response

Each person responds differently to crisis. The individuality of response depends upon having observed others in crisis or upon past personal experience. Some who show a calm personality before disease may become hysterical in the face of minor health problems. The emotionally unstable person may be the "rock," the calm foundation who must weather the storm for the family.

It appears that a person's "crisis personality" is constructed from a number of different pieces: learned behaviors, character traits, surrounding emotional support, ability to tolerate pain and suffering, and spiritual maturity. Thus it is both

| Category | Per 100,000 | Percent |
|---|---|---|
| 1) Diseases of the heart | 337.2 | 39 |
| 2) Malignant neoplasms (cancer) | 175.8 | 16 |
| 3) Cerebrovascular diseases | 87.9 | 12 |
| 4) Accidents | 46.9 | 7 |
| 5) Influenza and pneumonia | 28.8 | 4 |

**Table 1**
**Causes of Death**[1,2]

unnecessary and improper to measure the personality or character qualities of an individual solely by ability to handle a crisis. Total loss of control in crisis may be viewed by some as an inadequate personality or lack of emotional strength, but this is an unfair judgment.

Collapse in emotional crisis should be understood as the breaking of a chain at the weakest link. An individual's character, surrounding emotional support and spiritual maturity may all be well-developed; but the weak link of a learned behavior, such as a mother's hysterical response to pain, may cause total collapse of the person in crisis.

Even the most mature Christians, those with rock-solid faith, can wither or crack under the stress of a personal health crisis or one within their family. Does that make them faithless Christians, unable to hold on to the promises of God? "Judge not lest ye be judged."

Finding that weak link—a daughter who observed her mother cry hysterically over minor problems, a personality that tends toward overly emotional responses, an intense, unreasonable fear of pain—can allow the patient to see an area of personal growth. Counseling the patient to understand this emotional "domino effect" will relieve the guilt and shame of a hysterical outburst in crisis.

The most common initial emotional response a conscious patient makes is that of denial. It is, as mentioned earlier, the first stage of the grieving response suggested by Dr. Elisabeth Kübler-Ross and others who have written about psychological reactions to illness. Denial is probably the most common defense mechanism for almost all painful, sudden situations people face.[3] On the night of Christ's arrest, when the apostle Peter was confronted with the accusation "you knew him," his response was denial (Matt. 26:69–75). Was he afraid of physical abuse by the crowd? Or was he denying the Savior he loved so much because he couldn't bear the thought of his capture and probable death? Was Peter's weak link his lack of faith in Christ or lack of confidence in himself? All are possible, normal, understandable responses.

Another form of denial includes the emotional acceptance of the facts with an apparent absence of emotional response. The individual may be denying the emotional response, thereby suppressing the initiation and potential resolution of the grieving process.

In a terminal illness, denial may serve a useful, therapeutic role and should be respected.[4] Denial appears to be counterproductive, however, in the patients who have a chance of recovery and rehabilitation: it keeps them from accepting reality and investing emotionally in a rehabilitation plan. Counsel the patient to break the denial mechanism only if it appears best in view of long-term recovery or if it will help the patient and family members deal with imminent death.

Other defense mechanisms help people cope with sudden loss of health or mounting pain. These defenses also appear in other life stages, in psychiatric illnesses, in the grief process, and to some extent in coping with normal stresses. The arsenal includes regression, suppression, rationalization, projection, repression, anxiety, ambivalence, and hostility.[5] The woman who has a hysterectomy after uterine cancer may subconsciously regress, becoming more self-centered, dependent, and childlike to protect herself from the pain of surgery and the emotional loss of her childbearing function. The middle-aged man who suffers a serious heart attack may talk excessively about anything, suppressing the possibility of having to think about death or the loss of his job. He may also rationalize that since his chest pain is gone, his heart attack was minor, and he should be back to work next week. The child who loses a leg to a bone tumor may project that it happened "because the boy down the hall needed one more than I did." The man just diagnosed as having a spinal tumor may attempt to repress his real condition by telling others that his back pain comes from a slipped disk.

## Emotional Response of Family

Victor was a robust man in his late fifties, a Christian who loved his church, serving in the choir and on the prayer committee. One night his wife came home from work to find him babbling in a chair, food all over his shirt and spittle dripping from the corner of his mouth. Tests at the emergency room showed that Victor had suffered a brain hemorrhage.

You could not find a calmer wife anywhere. She cleaned him

up, transferred him to the car, and drove quickly, but cautiously, to the hospital. She watched over him during the exams and tests, took the diagnosis with grace, shed a few tears, and made the pronouncement "I'll do everything I can to help him recover."

Things were going well. For about a week Victor seemed to be recovering his speech and his walking ability. And then more bleeding occurred in the brain, and all the symptoms had recurred.

That appeared to be the breaking point for Victor's wife. She went into a tirade in the neurologic Intensive Care Unit: the nurses were feeding him incorrectly and walking him too much; the physicians were giving him the wrong medications, and the hospital was too substandard to cure anyone. Projections of blame, rationalizations, and suppressive thoughts were all reactions to prevent her from having to deal with the truth—the severity and certainty of loss to the husband she loved.

Family reactions to acute illness also begin with denial of the health problem and the circumstances that led to it. The mother who states, "My son could not have been in a car accident because he was at a friend's birthday party" denies and rationalizes why it cannot be her child in the intensive care unit. Denial can become so strong that a family member retreats into isolation. This hurts the patient by drawing the familial support system to the denying member instead of to him. The young woman caught in the throes of denial may refuse to visit the hospital and see her dying brother. The brother is tragically without his closest sibling, to touch, to receive comfort and encouragement, because of her pathological denial.

Transferring blame to other victims of an accident, to past situations, to physicians or to health-care providers is also a common defense mechanism that supports the denial of painful reality. Apparent apathy about the seriousness of the problem suggests suppression of the grief response. Guilty feelings, hostile reactions, or physical symptoms of illness often manifest themselves during the acceptance process as a means of distraction. Almost any emotional response can be seen as a family begins to react to illness, even emotions as inappropriate as elation and joy.

How does the counselor sort through these rapidly changing, confusing, and often inappropriate responses to help others adjust to devastating physical, emotional and spiritual testings?

## THE COUNSELOR'S ROLE

The family drives immediately to the hospital upon receiving the dreaded phone call. After finding out the condition and needed therapies, family members often phone their support system—pastor, extended family, and close friends. Seldom does this initial support system include a professional counselor, psychologist, or psychiatrist. The pastor will often be called early in the acute crisis to offer spiritual and psychological support for the family and victim. Accessibility is the key for developing a ministry to those with serious physical needs—they have to be able to reach you within a few hours.

The first hours or days after the accident are seldom deeply therapeutic times. "Putting out brush fires" may be the best terminology for counseling the acutely ill and their families. Emotions will vacillate, defense mechanisms will rapidly melt into open sobbing. Decisions that may hold life or death in the balance will need to be made as rapidly as possible. This is obviously not the time to accomplish any effective measure of long-term psychotherapy for deep family or emotional problems.

The Great Physician himself, Jesus, had the opportunity to minister during many serious health crises. Despite the limited information Scripture gives about his counseling techniques, we can learn from his words. In Luke 8:41–56 he gives comfort to Jairus:

> While Jesus was still speaking, someone came from the house of Jairus, the synagogue ruler. "Your daughter is dead," he said. "Don't bother the teacher any more."
> Hearing this, Jesus said to Jairus, "Don't be afraid; just believe, and she will be healed." (NIV)

Jesus spoke words of comfort and hope to a grieving father, a man whose thoughts now raced between "my daughter is dead" and "Jesus says, 'Believe.'"

When he arrived at the home of Jairus, the Lord attempted to calm and encourage family and friends. "Stop wailing," Jesus said. "She is not dead but asleep."

Notwithstanding the laughing comments of the "mourners," the mother and father were distracted from the reality of death to hope their daughter would be healed.

This Scripture illustrates the two key needs that should be addressed in an acute health crisis: encouragement and distraction. The longer-term emotional reactions of the grieving process can be dealt with as the acute situation stabilizes and specific facts about the illness are digested.

The usual pastoral tasks—holding a hand, touching a shoulder, praying with the family for the victim's healing, praying for strength and courage for the bereaved, reading appropriate Scripture, helping with communication to others—all these caring gestures offer hope and encouragement. These activities also distract thoughts away from the emotional pain.

Once the acute crisis has stabilized or the intensity of the situation has relaxed, then a longer-term therapeutic relationship can be established to deal with other issues. Is there inappropriate denial, persistent anger or bitterness, physical and emotional regression? The vulnerability of a crisis situation may bring many of these unresolved emotional conflicts to the surface for later handling.

But both patient and family need support and distraction first. As medical information begins to reach the patient, and as diagnosis and treatments are being finalized, the counselor may become involved with other therapeutic tasks. These include fostering expectations of recovery, guiding the decision-making process, acting as an information intermediary, and helping to make sure the physical, psychological, and spiritual needs of the family are met.

## Fostering Expectations of Recovery

The second patient I saw in my professional career was a seventy-two-year-old coal miner who was complaining of coughing up mucous and blood. As it turned out, he not only had a lung cancer, but he had known about it for almost a year and had neglected to get treatment. He was then referred for palliative radiation therapy that would relieve symptoms without curing the cancer.

He did fairly well through his first year. On two occasions he developed pneumonia, but each was easily treated. The good news kept coming back—no recurrence of tumor, anywhere.

Fourteen months after his radiation therapy he was admitted to the hospital—weak, short of breath, and having some chest discomfort. After searching diligently, we could find only very small metastasis to bone. There was no scientific way to account for why he was on death's doorstep. After attempting to encourage him with all the good news and becoming very frustrated by his continued deterioration, I discussed my patient with one of our faculty.

"It is apparent that he is just giving up," he said. "He just wants to die, and there is nothing you can do to stop him."

Even with my encouragement about his good medical report, attempts to talk with him about his feelings, and every supportive gesture I could give, he gave only his typical response. He didn't say a word and stared at the window.

He did die about two weeks after admission. We reported the cause of death as respiratory failure, but it should have been an "unshakeable will to die."

Since this initial patient, I've seen half a dozen people whose medical condition did not warrant death when it actually happened. The only reasonable explanation is that they willed to die. Many Christians believe only God holds that power in his hands. Although I will gladly leave this debate to theologians better versed in the arguments for free will versus predestination, a will to die does make sense physiologically—emotional suppression of the healing functions can lead to death.[6]

Knowing that a strong will to die or not get better affects the body's ability to recover from an illness, the counselor should foster a positive outlook toward the illness, rehabilitation, and recovery. Those with a positive attitude toward illness improve their immune system's function—their ability to heal—and will rehabilitate more quickly and recover more completely.

We can foster a positive outcome when we gain knowledge about the patient's condition. If the physician has permission to give you information about the illness, then you will be able to pass this along to the patient and his or her family. Stressing the positive, hopeful aspects of the illness—how much better the patient is compared to others, how quickly the patient is recovering—all give needed hope and encouragement. Researching the illness and its complications through a lay-level medical encyclopedia can enable the counselor to encourage with knowledge.[7] The more knowledge you possess, the more the patient and family will trust your positive encouragement.

If confronted with a patient who has low expectations about his or her disease, the counselor may want to use one of the following strategies to foster higher expectations. Openly discuss the biochemical causes of depression and the "death wish" that it may bring. Ask about specific reasons for the patient's low expectations (self-pity, guilt, lack of support). Find out what are the most beloved objects, pets, persons, or activities. To the best of your ability, attempt to bring these to the patient in hope of changing his or her desires. You may be able to break the patient's cycle of self-pity and hopelessness by asking him or her to pray and become concerned about the needs of other friends, family members or Christian brothers and sisters.

Should the counselor attempt to change the mind of a mature Christian who, at death's door, desires "eternal fellowship with the Savior"? It is not difficult to distinguish those who are folding from self-pity or biochemical depression from those who see death as a huge step forward. Supporting their desire of heaven and distraction from pain or other complications should be the task of the caring Christian counselor. I have said to more than one dying believer, "I wish that I could go with you."

> And God shall wipe away all tears from their eyes; and there shall be no more death, neither sorrow, nor crying, neither shall there be any more pain.  (Rev. 21:4)

## Guiding the Decision-Making Process

An acute health crisis may be the most disrupting force in the decision-making process. Few, if any, patients or families are good decision-makers when it comes to the complex choices offered in our medical environments. The counselor may become the most objective person in a family's support system, helping members make sure their decisions are made on the basis of information, logic, common sense, and Scripture, instead of on the basis of feelings alone.

The counselor must not, however, become the decision maker. Professional liability considerations and ethical problems will haunt those who do. If the counselor decides to take on that responsibility because the family is unwilling to make important decisions, then appropriate guardianship or durable power-of-attorney must be obtained first.[8]

Rational decisions based on information, logic, common sense and the principles of Scripture are decisions that will benefit the patient. Counselors may suggest to the family that the pros and cons of each decision be weighed against the expected outcomes. Gaining as much information as possible about the disease and the patient's situation may appear to complicate the decision, but the process usually clarifies portions of the decision if not all of it.[9] Applying Scripture to the decision is often difficult for the family. It should be offered when the counselor sees some spiritual insight to be gained from a given text or principle.

I have used a decision pathway based on Scripture for difficult medical and ethical decisions. The family can use this pathway for difficult health-care decisions when an illness creates confusion. It is called the *compassion-sacrifice-obedience* pathway. Here are two examples.

The Moores had been looking forward to the delivery of their "middle-age" child since conception. Their expectations were crushed at delivery. All of a sudden, they were dealing with a retarded, Downs Syndrome child and difficult decisions that they had to make to save his life.

At birth, the baby had the typical features of Downs Syndrome: He was blue and stayed that way. He choked whenever any feedings were given. The physicians told them surgery was necessary for the child to survive, but they strongly recommended against it because of his "low quality of life." This couple had heard stories of the misery a Downs Syndrome child brings to a family. But they were sure God was too wise to make a mistake. They didn't want the baby to suffer through the surgery only to see him suffer much more in the days to come.

After collecting as much information as possible, they applied the *compassion-sacrifice-obedience* decision tree to their possibilities.

Was it more *compassionate* to allow the child to die, removing food and water, or to give the child a chance to live a sheltered, but healthy life? Compassion suggested to them that "a chance" was better than starvation.

Was it more *sacrificial* for the family to allow the child to die (relieving them of future family discomfort) or more sacrificial to stand with the baby through surgery, through recovery, and through a potentially difficult life? It was more sacrificial to ask for the surgery.

Were they *obedient* to Scripture by depriving their child of food, water, life, hope, and a chance to have a simple, but happy, life by protecting and caring for the child God gave them? Obedience to Scripture suggested the long-term care of the child.

The Moores chose surgery and were rewarded with a mildly retarded child who grew up to work in a sheltered workshop, loved his family and had a good quality of life. Michael trusted in Jesus for his salvation at the age of eighteen.

The Candlers also faced a difficult decision—whether to put their mother in a nursing home after a serious stroke or to care for her themselves.

*Compassion* suggested that they try to care for her at home, in an environment where she could be a part of the family. But because of the severity of the stroke, she was probably not aware of much that occurred around her. Home nursing care was unavailable; and the complexities of the physical therapy, the medications, the Foley catheter, and other problems made constant access to a nurse the more compassionate choice.

It was more *sacrificial* to keep the mother in the home since she required constant care. Doing so, however, might neglect some needs of the family. But *obedience* to Scripture strongly suggested that the child's responsibility is to care for the parent if at all possible.

The decision was made to give home nursing a try. It quickly became apparent that the medical situation was more demanding than first anticipated, and it actually endangered the mother's health to keep her at home. But the family kept her until her death, anyway, because of a statement found in her written directions about funeral arrangements—"I would be happiest to die with my family around me, just as my mother died in the presence of her loved ones."

Sacrifice and obedience to "obey thy mother" became the most compassionate way to care for her even though home care probably hastened her death. Her wishes were followed as closely as the family could follow them.

These qualities are three of the highest spiritual qualities that God desires to see in all human relationships. It makes sense that these should be the highest qualities of any decision that we make for another person or for our families. They do not always yield a clear answer. Two families facing similar situations may decide differently using this method. That is to be expected. But when some families are making life-or-death decisions on the basis of convenience, a bank account, or pleasure, a more biblically measured approach can do nothing but help.

Decisions we make for other family members will be selfish and hurtful if we take only our comfort into account. Decisions based on compassion for the ill person, self-sacrifice to help the wounded, and obedience to the principles of Scripture will undoubtedly be the best ones in God's eyes.

## Acting as an Information Intermediary

Praying for God's will and guidance in a difficult time of decision-making is essential, but it may not always yield a clear solution to the problem. At such a time, information about the disease and the patient—from the physician or from other health resources—can help the family make a decision that is not based solely on emotion. Counselors who act as information collectors must allot sufficient time for telephone calls, talking with nurses and therapists, and investigating other information sources.

They should regularly collect health information from articles in magazines, newspapers, books, and medical encyclopedias. These aids will give the counselor a ready reference of the latest health information that can be tapped to meet the family's needs. Ask health professionals in your congregation or sphere of friends to be "on call" for health questions. Also, be aware of the numerous information organizations—the American Heart Association, the American Cancer Society, and others responsible for long-term care programs, general information, and support groups.[10] The counselor who uses these information resources, at little or no cost, can save a family from a costly, errant decision.

Try to pass this information to one key family member. Arrange to have that person available to receive your collected information about the disease, the patient's condition, test results, necessary therapies, and any change in prognosis. The family member should be able to relay this information accurately to the others in the family. The fewer times this information is passed, the more likely it will be accurate.

In our information age, the task of collecting complicated information, digesting it and simplifying it for the family represents an exceptional service to those to whom you minister.

### Supporting the Family

Being aware of the many needs of a family in crisis and being able to help meet them goes beyond the traditional responsibilities of the pastor or counselor. Christ did not neglect physical needs (feeding the thousands), emotional needs (encouraging Mary and Martha at the death of Lazarus), or spiritual needs of those within his ministry. Organizing groups of "mercy-showers" who will help meet these needs in times of crisis allows the pastor or counselor to extend the hands of the congregation to the hurting.

For instance, the physical needs may be for shelter for those who come from a distant town or food for a family constantly at the bedside. The pastor or counselor can organize people in the congregation to house friends and relatives at such times. Congregation members can deliver meals to those recovering from an illness or grieving the death of a loved one. People in the church could be called to fix lunches that need no refrigeration and can be used as snacks for family or visiting friends.

From the spiritual aspect, prayer is the most important support a Christian family could ever receive from its pastor or congregation. Other spiritual helps are also useful: taping a service, giving a family reading material on grieving or dealing with illness, making a radio or tape player available. Each of these offers a spiritual uplift and distraction from pain. Just spending time with the patient or family, listening or talking about church, about Bible studies, about a good Christian book (or reading the book to them) are excellent ways to be a spiritual help.

God can show the counselor many other ways to help as he or she seeks to serve in meeting the physical, emotional, and spiritual needs of those suffering.

## COMA AND COUNSELING

Science is still bewildered by the interface between life and death, by the transition from the soul merged with the body to the soul "floating" freely in the room. A number of accounts by those whose hearts have stopped say that they were floating above the body, watching and hearing everything in the room but feeling no pain. Then a firm voice tells them "not yet," and they immediately awaken in the body they just left. They feel an undeniable "peace, a lack of pain and fear."[11] Is this a dream? Is this experience, often called a "near-death" or "out-of-body" experience, an actual separation of the soul and the body? Or is it some hoax to gain attention?

There are too many unanswered questions and no way to answer them. In my practice, I have discussed near-death situations with about five people. Each described it as a painless, peaceful situation, until they returned to the body. None of them was seeking attention. All were amazed at the sensations of quietly floating in an unknown transition.

This scientific zone between life and death is often called a coma. Many describe a comatose person as one who cannot respond to pain, to words, or to his or her environment. Many people in a coma are aware of activity, talking, or personal care but are unable to respond. Some have said they could hear, but they could not see or move.

Physicians need very specific information about the function and damage that occurs in a coma. This led to the development of the Glasgow Coma Scale, a widely used method of grading the ability of the patient's nervous system to respond to the environment. A patient with a score of fifteen will be conscious, responsive to commands, and able to look around the room. A person in the deepest stages of a coma will have a score of three—no response to surroundings.

How the counselor or family should approach the comatose patient depends upon the level of coma and (as shown in Table 2) the type of responses observed. Eye responses may be the best indicator that the patient understands the comfort and support offered by family or counselor. Spontaneous opening of the eyes when people are talking in the room—especially looking toward the sound—is a good indicator of some cognizance of the meaning of conversation. Even when the patient cannot speak, "yes" or "no" communication is possible with eye movements.

Even if the patient appears to have no ability to understand and no response, it is still wise for the counselor, family, or medical staff not to talk about the patient's condition while in the room. Many people who have recovered report that they could hear what was said about them while comatose.

| Type of Response | Score |
|---|---|
| *Best Motor Response* | |
| Obeys commands | 6 |
| Localizes pain | 5 |
| Withdraws from pain | 4 |
| Flexion response to pain | 3 |
| Extension response to pain | 2 |
| No response | 1 |
| *Best Verbal Response* | |
| Oriented | 5 |
| Confused speech | 4 |
| Inappropriate speech | 3 |
| Incomprehensible speech | 2 |
| No speech | 1 |
| *Best Eye Response* | |
| Spontaneous | 4 |
| To command | 3 |
| To pain | 2 |
| No movement | 1 |

**Table 2**
**Glasgow Coma Scale**

Even when it appears that the patient is totally unresponsive, normal supportive communication from the family and counselor should be encouraged. Holding the hand, gentle touching of a shoulder, positive words of encouragement, reading Scripture, praying, or just making normal conversation may be welcomed by the patient. Talking to the patient in front of other family members as if he or she is awake and alert builds hope in total recovery.

The most predictive medical test used to ascertain brain function is the electroencephalogram (EEG). If it records no activity, little chance for recovery exists apart from a miracle of God. The more electrical activity seen, the more likely a full recovery. Knowing about EEG activity will help the counselor comfort the family and guide their expectations about recovery.

Some state laws now oblige the physician to turn off all life-support measures if there is an absence of brain-wave activity for three consecutive days. The assumption is that a rapid deterioration in the heart and lungs will ensue and lead to death.

All aspects of help ministries are necessary when an illness-producing coma occurs. The pastor or counselor will be called upon to help with "brush-fire" counseling: encouraging, praying, calling for food and shelter, and, most importantly, being available to listen. It is a time-consuming ministry, but it allows the privilege of growing in a trusting, intimate pastoral relationship that will reward patients, their families, and the counselor.

# CHAPTER SIX

## COUNSELING THE CHRONICALLY ILL

Sometimes when pain seems constant, when it becomes harder and harder to bear, when the strength to keep living seems gone, a question will nag at the back of the mind—is the effort really worthwhile?

Mrs. Laning always encouraged many people at her church. A pastor's wife, she had lost her husband from a heart attack about fifteen years earlier. She still grieved, but with a joyful heart, knowing they would be spending eternity with their Savior. At the age of eighty-two, she had every right to desire to go Home to be with him—but the Lord still needed her for some further work.

A year earlier a couple of medical problems had seemed to

sap Mrs. Laning's strength. On her way to the physician's office, she collapsed and was taken to the local hospital. A bladder and kidney infection had precipitated a more serious situation—a stroke. The blood clot that affected her brain knocked out some of her speech and all coordination and strength on the left side of her body. After two months of hospitalization and rehabilitation, she was transferred to a local nursing home.

Many people in such cases become bitter with God and ask why they couldn't simply have died. Not Mrs. Laning. She remained the sweet, encouraging, uplifting person who gave more than she took.

She had to return to the hospital when an infection around the gall bladder threatened her life. Yet, as she sat in her bed, in obvious pain, she continued to smile and show concern for others more than herself.

"How's your sick child?" she would ask a visitor.

Friends would comment on her beaming smile, her joyous tone of voice, her arms outstretched for a hug. When they saw how badly off she was, unable to walk or get out of bed, they were greatly encouraged by her. She was filled with God's love and Spirit, even though she was in desperate physical shape. People would say, "God has used her greatly in my life just by seeing her!"

Many of us wonder how God can use a severe chronic illness—such as a stroke, cancer, heart failure, or arthritis—to accomplish anything for his kingdom. Why does God allow the mental and physical deterioration of a stroke and the severe changes it can create in personality and ability to function? How can God use the painful, slow, agonizing death from a cancer that eats away at the body? What purpose is there in the shortness of breath and inability to walk or function that results from heart failure? How can people praise God for the unrelenting stiffness and discomfort of a crippling arthritis? It only takes a few examples like Mrs. Laning to see how God would like us to mature through our weakness, to trust him through our helplessness. We are reminded by Paul's thorn in the flesh that God can use weaknesses to His glory (2 Cor. 12:9).

Statistics show that the population of adults over sixty-five years of age continues to grow. In the United States, the elderly now comprise 11.3 percent of the total population.[1] Consequently, more people will be afflicted with long-term malfunctional or degenerative diseases that are often either incurable or only marginally treatable. Our churches reflect this same trend toward aging: Most of the financial support of larger ministries and churches comes from people older than fifty-five years of age. Individuals in this group are often caught in the chronic process of illness and its psychological and spiritual consequences.

## THE CHRONIC HEALTH PROCESS

Any illness that lingers longer than six months can be considered chronic. Although many infectious diseases are long gone within this time frame, the newly discovered "slow-virus" group, which includes the AIDS virus, is an exception. Most malfunctional diseases persist for life after their onset in the patient's forties, fifties, sixties, or later. Most degenerative conditions also begin later in life and remain until death, as shown in Table 3.

Most diseases treated in Western societies today are considered chronic. Here are some brief cases.

It has been years since Mr. Charles has been free of lung infection. A smoker in his youth, he was also afflicted with allergic asthma. Ever since his late fifties, he has had one infection after another. Physicians have told him that his smoking has led to emphysema and chronic bronchitis. He currently takes

| Disease | Percent of Persons Over 65 Affected |
|---|---|
| Heart disease | 34.0 |
| Cancer | 14.9 |
| Cerebrovascular disease | 13.4 |
| Pneumonia | 3.8 |
| Lung disease | 2.7 |
| Atherosclerosis | 2.6 |
| Diabetes Mellitus (elderly onset) | 1.8 |

**Table 3**
**List of Chronic Diseases[2]**

three lung medications and an inhaler every two hours. He uses oxygen day and night and almost always is taking one or two different antibiotics. He is constantly short of breath and has lost thirty pounds in the last year alone.

As his lung disease progresses, he becomes more bitter, more angry, more difficult to control. His bitterness is aimed at himself because he could not stop smoking. His family takes the brunt of this unpleasant demeanor and language, but they have rationalized it as "brain deterioration from too little oxygen."

Wendy has had cerebral palsy since birth. She has had to deal with the stigma of talking and walking "strangely" ever since first grade, but she has handled it well. She was able to graduate from college at the age of thirty-two with a degree in psychology, desiring to finish a master's in counseling.

Her family began rejecting her openly at the age of 10. They wouldn't drive her places, would not be seen with her, and often refused help with the wash or making the bed. Her father divorced her mother shortly after this rejection started, claiming he couldn't take living with this "freak." This only added to the rest of the family's rejection. To this day, her father refuses to help financially. He never writes and usually talks to her only when she calls first.

These emotional traumas and her cerebral palsy have pushed Wendy to be overly dependent upon people. She often manipulates them to help with simple tasks she can do for herself. She is constantly depressed, takes antidepressants, and cries when anything goes wrong. She can always make a disaster out of any success.

A few months ago, her father called and said he was going to be traveling through the state. He would stop by to see her for a few hours. She was very excited at first. Then she became apprehensive. A friend told her that cerebral palsy victims often die at the age of forty because of lung problems. Worry about the visit and the lung problems so upset Wendy that she developed shortness of breath and chest tightness. This did not remit with simple therapy in the emergency room, and she was admitted to the hospital. She did not improve with the usual medications, and it wasn't until after her father's fifteen-minute visit that she began to mend rapidly.

These cases illustrate the often difficult nature of chronic disease. These people live with constant reminders of their physical problems. To survive, they must find ways to cope with their illness, forget the unfairness, and distract themselves from their pain and inabilities. Christians must cope with their feelings about why a loving God could allow this to happen to them.

## THE PSYCHOLOGICAL RESPONSE OF PATIENTS

The typical response to crisis would include denial, irrational constructs, suppression of fact, wide swings of emotional outbursts, and use of emotional defenses. The response of patients to a slowly increasing, chronic, unrelenting illness can be quite different. It represents an individual's attempt to cope with the finer degrees of loss—loss of function, loss of purpose, loss of control, and loss of self-esteem.

The changes that occur in the individual are a complex overlapping of the seriousness of the illness, the degree of impairment, and the rate of functional losses. Complicating these are personality traits, psychological stability, spiritual maturity, and the depth of the local support system. For example, a middle-aged woman diagnosed with diabetes mellitus may have no significant emotional reaction because both her parents are affected and she needs only to change her diet. This early appearance of a minor chronic disease would bring a markedly different emotional reaction if the disease were more severe. The following case is an example.

A gentleman in his sixties had just lost his sight, been on kidney dialysis for three months, suffered a minor stroke, and begun taking three injections of insulin a day. His wife had died three years earlier, and his family had to place him in a nursing home because of the care he needed. Frequently he had crying spells. He would yell at the nursing staff, often telling them, "I would be better dead."

One day the nurse was called away while she was in the process of shaving this gentleman. He had enough time to pull the blade from the razor, slash both wrists and both jugular veins. By the time she returned, he was already in shock and died before reaching the hospital.

*113*

Emotional reactions, the first phase of the Unified Theory of Grief, are similar whether the illness is acute, the beginning of a chronic process, or an exacerbation of a chronic process. The initial phase occurs when the first symptoms become evident, tests are accomplished and a diagnosis is reached. Typical responses may include denial, rationalization, repression, regression, and suppression. Although these may be less pronounced in a chronic illness because of the length of adjustment the patient is afforded, emotional instability and irrational behavior may still result from the intense worsening of a chronic situation.

After the initial emotional reactions are played out, the cognitive processes take over and the acceptance phase is near. The patient reassesses role, purpose, support system, and self-esteem.[3] Hopefully, this takes little time and effort. Usually with small increments of physical symptoms, increases in the emotional responses are minor, and reassessment and acceptance are rapid. This opens the door for a positive attitude toward the care, and emotional and cognitive acceptance of the illness make rehabilitation possible.

Why do so many patients disregard a physician's advice concerning the importance of long-term, fastidious care for many diseases, such as diabetes, hypertension and arthritis? Why do they shirk their personal responsibilities when they are sure of suffering the consequences in the future?

Patients will often be caught in denial, falsely believing that these chronic processes are curable.[4] They would rather postpone their own responsibilities and believe that "God will cure it very soon." This only guarantees failure because without proper care, the disease quickly worsens. When a patient's hope for a magical cure dissolves into worse disease, the losses grow more quickly, and the fall is more emotionally vicious.

Early counseling by the physician often fails in these cases. It falls on the shoulders of the counselor to help such patients understand that their desire for instantaneous cure has worsened their condition. Breaking through this denial phase is essential before patients become psychologically and physically shattered. Chronically ill patients must accept the ups and downs of each illness and the responsibility to care for their long-term rehabilitation until "the Lord heals them."

"Sure I accept my hypertension. I have no anger," a patient may say. But that may not mean he is willing to take his medication, have his blood pressure checked, see the eye specialist or follow through with his physician visits. It becomes the counselor's ministry to guide these patients into healthy adaptive behaviors for coping with their suffering. It is also important to dissuade patients from using such maladaptive mechanisms as manipulative behavior, convenience regression, inappropriate anger, coercion, or hypochondria.

Maladaptive mechanisms are often seated deep within the patient's personality as learned behaviors. The typical hysteric, for example, is often a female with multiple medical problems. She learns her hypochondriacal, manipulative behavior pattern from her mother's behavior throughout many illnesses.[5] Hysterics use this behavior to rally their family support system. If the counselor proves that there is no disease, this may cause a complete psychotic break. In these people, illness, manipulation, and hypochondriacal behavior are all necessary for the maintenance of reality.

Other maladaptive behaviors may be equally as important to the personality structure of the ill. An embittered, overworked caregiver may see her opportunity to play up an illness for all it is worth. She may moan, groan, demand constant attention and act like an ill four-year-old. This patient has regressed from the behavior of an adult to fulfill her dependency needs.

An elderly man may use anger and threats to achieve his needs or desires when he sees his caregivers failing to respond to less emphatic types of communication. The arthritic who withdraws from church, activities, and friendships is coping with her deforming joint changes in a maladaptive, non-supportive environment.

In each of these maladaptive situations, the counselor must help patients gain insight into their needs and their coping methods. He or she can describe other adaptive, healthy methods that will help to pull patients from their defensive shells. But counseling will likely fall on deaf ears if the counselor uses direct confrontation and directive styles. These seldom work with chronically ill patients because they have developed stubbornness as one of their chief defenses.

What are the healthy, adaptive mechanisms used by the chronically ill patient?

Normal adaptive mechanisms for physical problems include planning for rehabilitation, careful and orderly compulsive behaviors, setting goals and charting progress, adapting to new physical aids, and decreasing physically difficult tasks. The individual who has completed the reaction and acceptance phases of an illness can use compulsive, orderly lifestyle changes to help cope with the rigors of decreased strength and physical therapy.

A healthy adaptation to a chronic illness also has spiritual signs. God intends for people to mature through acute and chronic sufferings. Saul was tested by a recurring mental illness, described as "fits" (possibly bouts of depression), that caused him to suffer. He called for music to calm this "tormenting spirit" (1 Sam. 16:14–17). Yet he neither repented nor sought God's forgiveness. Job, on the other hand, matured through testings of his emotional and spiritual losses. He grew to trust God more completely and to understand his character more fully. God restored to him all that he had lost—and much more (Job 42:12). Saul refused to accept both the loss of his kingdom and God's correction through the illness process. Job accepted his losses and God's sovereignty in all things.

The chronic suffering, depression, and exhaustion that pain creates are not likely to prompt people to praise God for their trials, but God desires to increase patience and faith through the trial of physical illness. What more profound tester exists than the slow, unrelenting torment of a chronic physical condition?

## COURSE AND EFFECT

Chronic illnesses are quite unpredictable. They wax and wane. They have plateaus with partial symptoms, or perhaps none at all. They have slow and rapid slides toward deterioration. The course of that deterioration depends upon the illness and the individual.

A progressively worsening illness causes the greatest amount of personality and emotional degeneration. No longer can patients deny the reason for the illness or rationalize that the situation is not worsening because they are doing everything "right." Since their families may not comprehend the increasing needs of these patients, they may feel more isolated and more helpless. A cherished role may be slipping from their hands.

A counseling session represents only a snapshot of a patient's psychological condition at one given moment. It changes constantly. With increasing pain and inability to function, patients may regress into a childlike world. If their physical, emotional, or spiritual reserves are depleted, a total collapse can occur. The needs, changes, and disease are so complex and interrelated that almost any combination of problems can surface. The counseling situation may parallel that of an acute illness, in which the pastor or counselor can deal only with the most urgent psychological needs.

The roller-coaster course acts constantly to keep a patient's emotional damage-control system off balance. Most patients with chronic disease fortunately have sufficient reserves to cope with the minor worsenings and plenty of time to adjust to new levels of disease. The counseling process with these people includes discussion of how they previously coped, patterns of change and readjustment they have established, present needs, healthy adaptation to disabilities, and changes in their support system. Don't forget to teach patients about the disease, the expected course, and the eventual outcomes—it will help to break the need for maladaptive defense mechanisms.

## FAMILY MECHANISMS FOR COPING WITH CHRONIC ILLNESS

The reactions of family members to chronic illness are diverse and complex. They can become a bewildering array of communication malfunctions, relationship alterations, and unfulfilled need patterns. Some patterns seen in these family structures, however, function to meet the health and emotional needs of the chronically ill patient. Dysfunctional patterns can also develop and may need to be dealt with through supportive counseling or through family counseling.

The family with a chronically ill, elderly adult often displays a regressive, protective structure. The patient regresses from a caregiving or leadership role to one of receiving care in a childlike manner. The family adjusts to the extra care responsibilities just as if another child were added to the family. They excuse foul language, overly demanding behavior, emotional outbursts, poor self-care, and other actions as the normal childlike regression of degenerative mental faculties. They may shield the patient from difficult situations, thus reinforcing his or her need for "parental protection." The patient's dependence upon his or her support system often grows to the point of personal and family dysfunction.

This regressive pattern is healthy initially, but it becomes dysfunctional when care demands exceed the time and family members available to meet them. The patient, because of physical or mental disabilities, grows increasingly dependent upon protection and care from others. The regressive, demanding behaviors unconsciously produce increased support.[6] Once the limit of tolerance for these behaviors is reached, the increasing demands may drive family members away from the patient instead of toward meeting new demands. Then the need to make alternate caretaking decisions, such as admission to a nursing home, often precipitates an emotional crisis.

The family should be counseled early to protect the patient from this spiral of increasing demands. Encourage the ill member to contribute to the family by helping with simple tasks, praying for other members, offering words of support, and caring for himself where appropriate. All such steps help to prevent overly demanding behavior.

The withdrawal reaction—a dysfunctional way for family members to protect and support their denial of chronic illness—may cause a dangerous situation for the patient.[7] The family members may not want to integrate patient care needs into its planning and daily activities. As a result, they may acquire a nearby apartment, add a wing or room to the house, or opt for a nursing home situation to maintain care outside of the family. The emotional protection that this offers the family is obvious: It perpetuates denial, postpones grief, and conveniently places guilt out of sight.

Withdrawal can also place patients at risk. When they are set aside from their support groups, emotional needs often go unmet. The patient may slide rapidly into depression, withdraw from the family, and sink into worsening physical problems.

Self-care apathy may lead to malnutrition, forgetting to take necessary medications, or a lack of personal hygiene. Patients' situations become dangerous when depression, apathy, and lack of self-care are not recognized by their families. Alienation and neglect of elderly patients has become a serious, ever-increasing problem in the United States.[8]

Counseling the family that has stopped caring for its chronically ill member involves the principles previously discussed for patients. Breaking the denial system through education and reality therapy is the initial goal.

We can help patients to renew trust and communication between themselves and their families by dealing with demanding behaviors that arouse anger and guilt. Offer alternative care options such as a weekend or vacation away from the patient. This helps prevent the family from feeling trapped by burdensome, constant care needs. Encourage the family to consider more supportive options that will allow the sick member to make emotionally substantial contributions to the home.

The family's reaction to a chronic illness may include portions of the grieving process, such as reassessment, acceptance, and resolution. The ultimate decision to care for its ill member may be aided by use of the compassion-sacrifice-obedience model discussed earlier. Consider an example.

When Ted had his heart attack, both he and the family went through an extremely emotional time of reassessment. Ted was earning about $250,000 per year as a professional athlete. The illness brought an abrupt end to his career and his contract.

His two teenage daughters were not very close to their father, but they were very close to the wealth, fame, and good times he brought. Their readjustment was initially difficult. Their hefty allowances were cut to almost nothing. Friends were left behind when they moved to less expensive housing. Their private school was now just a memory. It was during this time of readjustment that the Holy Spirit convicted their hearts through a Billy Graham Crusade broadcast, and both became believers. They traded their hatred for "what Dad did to himself" to "I want to know and love Dad more." Their hatred and frustration with the circumstances also melted into a closer relationship with their mother.

As a professional athlete, Ted had the most difficult time. His role in the family changed drastically, his self-esteem fell apart, and his financial future seemed bleak because everyone had overspent. His world was crashing in around him, so he desperately attempted to deny the seriousness of the illness—even though one-third of his heart was destroyed by the blood clot. A title to fame and self-esteem as one of the "best in the world" was his no longer.

Ted covered the seriousness of the situation with denial. He used reaction formation to lessen its impact, but inside he was boiling with guilt, anger, and frustration. He knew he had been a poor father to his two daughters. He knew the possibility of death would place "his sin" on the highest, most prominent billboards. He began to pray for God's help to survive.

Ted's wife remained strong during the entire episode. Her faith in Christ had given her a firm foundation, and the earlier death of her mother had tested and proved it. She kept encouraging Ted, helping him to understand the full impact of the heart attack and the changes they would have to make in their lifestyles. While Ted was still in the hospital, she made all the arrangements to move, to sell what was unnecessary, and to refinance loans to greatly reduce their debt. She also made sure that their pastor visited Ted daily, spending from one to two hours just talking about the changes and God's sovereignty. A "man's man" was unlikely to take any advice from a woman, let alone his own wife, she felt.

It seemed like Ted had accepted his illness about the same time his daughters became believers. He could see the positive changes in them, and this helped greatly to reinforce his desire to put the heart attack behind him and start rehabilitation.

The next six months was a beautiful time as family members grew to love and encourage each other while they helped Dad with his walking, dietary changes, and medication. They became a solid, functioning unit. Communication was excellent and feelings were shared openly. The centerpiece of the success was obviously the spiritual dimension that had been restored to the family. Their consistent prayer for each other, family devotions, and church attendance gave them a reason to hope for Ted's complete recovery.

Ted's family and their reaction to his long-term illness is ideal in two ways. It is an excellent example of a family working through its initial defense mechanisms to become a strongly coherent unit that supports the rehabilitation and restoration of its chronically ill leader. It is also an example of God's ministry—restoration, salvation of daughters, rededication of Ted, growth and maturation of all—through the testing from physical illness. God's timing is always perfect, and the testing allowed is always the proper amount.

Prevention, of course, is the best and most inexpensive cure for any disease process. If a person starts to deal with a problem as soon as it begins to surface, emotional reactions can be dealt with long before communication breaks down. The counselor should take a good emotional history of the family: communication patterns, expectations of the illness, fears and anxieties, roles and family structure, and any current dysfunctional relationships. This will give a knowledge base from which to work and provide the tools to prevent further emotional entanglements. If the spiral of family dysfunction (failed defense mechanisms leading to negative emotional expressions leading to poor physical recuperation) is not broken, more serious psychiatric consequences can surface.

## PSYCHIATRIC COMPLICATIONS OF CHRONIC ILLNESS

The severity of an acute change in condition, coupled with the constant stress and fatigue created by chronic illness, may lead to psychiatric complications requiring medical or hospital therapy. The risk factors that increase the chances of serious psychiatric complications include a family history of psychiatric illness, an obvious overwhelming of defense mechanisms, multiple emotional traumas within a short time, present or previous illness, use of psychiatric medications, and the absence of a viable support system.[9] Early recognition of these risk factors (and the early signs of depression, suicide, dysfunctional families, anxieties, or psychosis) will allow for swifter treatment and recovery.

In today's legal environment, swift recognition of these cues is important for the counselor or pastor actively involved in hospital or office-based counseling of the chronically ill. Referral

to a psychiatrist or physician familiar with psychiatry is important as well.

## Depression

Physical illness places extreme demands upon the nervous
system of the ill person—primarily through hormonal and biochemical stress mechanisms. These affect all areas of the brain,
causing fatigue, decreased mental acuity, and reduced motivation and desire. Stress hormones appear to play a large role
in the biochemical changes seen in depression. The emotional
factors—decreased self-esteem, losses of role, abilities, and control, disruption of communication and support systems—all de-
plete the individual's stores of hope. Even simple, short-term
illness will lead to temporary depression through these same
biochemical mechanisms.

Depression needs to be recognized before it becomes immo-
bilizing or leads to the fatal consequence of suicide. In most
cases, treatment with antidepressant medications proves successful. Not only is suicide averted, but the physical and emotional symptoms of depression are also lifted.[10] A wonderful side
effect often seen with use of antidepressant medications is a
lessening of chronic pain's severity.

A person sliding into the depths of depression may exhibit
emotional and physical symptoms. A list of both types includes:[11]

- poor appetite or significant weight loss.
- insomnia or hypersomnia.
- psychomotor retardation or agitation.
- loss of interest or pleasure in usual activities, including a
  decrease in sexual drive.
- loss of energy or fatigue.
- feelings of worthlessness, self-reproach or inappropriate
  guilt.
- decreased concentration, indecisiveness.
- recurrent thoughts of death or suicidal ideation.

As counselors help their patients reverse the trend toward
depression, they can use these two simple examples to help them
deal with any guilt and shame.

1. I have often explained to patients, whether depressed or recovering from psychotic illnesses, that these illnesses may be just like the diseases caused by hormonal deficiencies, diabetes or hypothyroidism. Low insulin, for example, causes blood-sugar changes that affect brain and body alike. Replacement of the hormone with insulin injections—or moderating the level of brain hormones with antidepressant medication—helps the body return to its normal patterns of emotions, energy, and sleep. Dealing with the precipitating factors—the psychological and emotional triggers—is also essential.

2. Physical and psychiatric diseases are allowed by God to test the afflicted individual and family. Epilepsy was once viewed as demon possession because it could not be explained. Now we understand that electrical short circuits of the brain cause the writhing and uncontrolled twisting of a seizure. Similarly, a paralyzing spinal cord injury is a disease involving disrupted electrical impulses from the brain to the rest of the body.

The scientific view of disease at the biochemical level has helped to discover rational treatments and guilt-relieving explanations for our patients. In most cases, however, other emotional aspects have complicated or initiated the disease, and they also must be addressed in counseling. It is malpractice to provide only counseling or only medication when the patient has need of both.

## Anxieties and Fears

Among the chronically ill, simple anxiety and rational fears may escalate into anxieties demanding medical treatment and irrational fears; they may also become psychosis and paranoia. Again, early recognition of the common physical and emotional symptoms of these disorders is the most effective way to promote resolution and prevent progression. A brief list of common symptoms includes:[12]

- anorexia, butterflies in stomach, nausea, vomiting.
- chest pains or tightness, hyperventilation.
- palpitations, shortness of breath, shakiness.
- feeling "about ready to explode inside."

- dizziness, dry mouth, headache, muscle tension.
- "crawling sensations" in the stomach, chest or extremities.

Since specific biochemical tranquilizers are available for anxieties and irrational fears, it is wise to tell patients that a biochemical problem may be at the root. The exact biochemical and hormonal causes are not yet clear, but a number of theories have been postulated. Most people displaying anxiety do not need medication, however, and counseling has by far the most to offer them when dealing with the stresses of life and disease in a non-functional way.

## CONFUSION/SENILITY OF DISEASE ORIGIN

Andrew's stay in the hospital was unusually lengthy, but for good reason. This eighty-six-year-old had been treated with an antibiotic after his surgery to prevent the possibility of infection. The more dosages of antibiotic he was given, the more confused and senile he became. Although the stress of surgery was supposed to be the cause for this rapid mental deterioration, he did not improve with time. Within two days of stopping the antibiotics, his fevers stopped and his confusion began to clear. Within a week he was as sane, as belligerent, and as friendly as ever.

Many factors can explain the acute or gradual onset of confusion or dementia in an elderly, chronically ill patient. Such conditions are not necessarily the "permanent" disorders of Alzheimer's or Organic Brain Syndrome. The extreme stress of surgery, mechanical ventilation, cardiac monitoring, or intensive care can all lead to "ICU psychosis"—a temporary, but spontaneously resolving, psychosis that is cured by transfer to a normal room. Medications of many sorts have been proven the culprits behind confusion during various therapies. Other physical therapies, such as blood transfusions or whirlpool baths, have also been known to precipitate acute confusion.

The following acronym gives many of these reversible causes for acute psychosis:[13]

D — Drugs
E — Emotional illness (including depression)

M — Metabolic or endocrine disorders (diabetes, thyroid, etc.)

E — Eye/Ear environmental deprivation (decreased sight, hearing)

N — Nutritional and neurologic conditions (strokes)

T — Tumors or trauma (concussion)

I — Infection

A — Alcoholism, anemia, atherosclerosis

It is important to reassure the family that a permanent psychiatric condition, such as dementia, is seldom the cause of the acute confusion that occasionally complicates an acute or chronic illness. Asking if the patient has just taken a new medication, or increased the dosage of an established medication, can be key information. Making sure the family communicates with the medical team will facilitate a more rapid search for the cause and resolution of the problem.

Psychiatric complications from any illness devastate a family and patient because of the stigma society places on such disorders—often because of fear and lack of understanding. We can help families cope with these temporary psychiatric illnesses through education and counseling. It may prevent the family from withdrawing from the ill member who needs their constant love and support.

Long-term psychiatric illness can bring severe stresses to the family that must constantly deal with its difficult behaviors and societal stigmas. Many principles already discussed also apply to counseling the family of the psychiatrically ill patient.

# CHAPTER SEVEN

# COUNSELING THE PSYCHIATRICALLY ILL

Late phone calls to a physician's home seldom bear good news. This call about Shandra was no different.

I had never met this young woman before I received an urgent call from the local crisis pregnancy home. It only took about two minutes on the phone to know what her problem was.

"She is telling everyone that she is going to kill herself and her baby unless she gets a room by herself and is left totally by herself," the director explained. "We were not told that she was a problem in the last home. They told us she wanted to leave for another home."

"Have you tried calming her down to obtain a medical or psychiatric history from her?" I asked.

The director said he could get no information from her. "And she is so totally unruly, I believe we will have to discharge her tonight to the care of her parents. We've been trying to reach them for hours to get their help." I could tell he was frantic.

Since her parents were unwilling to help and she had stated openly her plan to commit suicide, we decided to admit this young mother to the local psychiatric ward for a cool-down period and counseling.

After about a day of anger, threats and general immature behavior (such as urinating on the carpet) we were able to talk with her. She had been admitted twice before to institutions, and her diagnoses had included depression, schizophrenia and manic-depressive illness. Medications routinely failed to help, although they usually were not given an adequate trial period. Her parents had arranged counseling for her with a psychiatrist, psychologist, pastor and mental health clinic, but they were not able to keep her going actively to any of them for treatment.

Her medical history was normal except for one abortion that was started with a coat hanger and completed at a hospital. Her self-destructive, manipulative behavior was obvious from both her past and her present.

Because of her pregnancy, we could not attempt to treat her medically. Her initial group and individual counseling was relatively successful in keeping her calm. When she could no longer dominate the group, however, she retreated to her room and threatened to kill her baby.

I called her parents, seeking verification of past medical and psychiatric problems. They said, "She is old enough to do for herself—we are not responsible for any bills." After I told them I was just trying to obtain information to better help their daughter, they quickly broke down and began to talk.

Shandra's parents confirmed her history and a few other episodes and details she had not shared with us. She once threatened her mother with a large kitchen knife and slashed a hole in her clothing. She had been arrested numerous times for drunken driving. She had used illegal drugs on many occasions in front of her parents and school authorities. On more than one occasion, she was treated for venereal infections, including herpes, at a local free clinic.

Her parents expressed mostly denial about her behavior. A local psychiatrist said they were not responsible for Shandra's psychiatric problems. But it became obvious during our conversation that Shandra's mother was domineering and often castigated her husband openly. Their discipline structure was non-existent, and the mother always blamed her daughter's rebellion on the lack of a "normal man in the home." This couple had been separated a number of times, often for six months or longer.

Shandra claimed she had accepted Christ at age eight or nine, and her parents also professed conversion many years earlier. But spiritual matters were never brought up in the home, and they rarely attended church because Shandra was always in trouble at school or with the law.

Almost all the statements about Shandra ended with an accusation of who was to blame for this or that behavior. Each parent pointed a finger at the other. But both also tried to vindicate themselves by stating that Shandra merely had "a chemical imbalance." Their guilt, frustration and grief were impossible to cover, and so was their anger, denial and shifting of blame.

It became apparent that the problem was not a short-term depression, but a long-term psychiatric illness that needed intensive inpatient care and family therapy. After five days Shandra went to a larger city hospital with a psychiatric division. I later heard that she walked out of that facility against medical advice and was admitted to another Christian maternity home.

Shandra's case demonstrates the complex interactions that bring about psychiatric illness and create further dysfunction and strife within the family. Shandra had developed an extremely maladaptive way to cry for help, a method patterned after her parent's dysfunctional blame-shifting, anger and denial. She became the object of her parents' anger and developed a hate toward herself that led to numerous self-destructive behaviors. Further problems with Shandra led to more marital disharmony, stronger anger, and blaming. A serious attempt to resolve the complex personality problems would have been difficult because Shandra's problems had become an integral part of the dysfunctional family structure.

Counselors or pastors must often face family problems associated with a psychiatric illness. They may be called upon to counsel the patient when other mental health avenues fail.

Any active counselor must be able to recognize psychiatric problems as early as possible. Then the patient can be channeled for appropriate medical therapy while continuing the counseling process. Building a relationship with a local Christian psychiatrist or family physician allows the counselor to make medical treatment referrals when necessary and to generate a second opinion on a strategy for counseling the patient. A strong professional relationship benefits both physician and counselor. The physician benefits from both the medical referral and the time gained as his colleague fulfills the counseling role for his patients. The counselor benefits by receiving medical backup, building a professional reputation and obtaining new counseling patients.

How can the counselor or pastor offer the greatest therapeutic help in treating psychiatric illness? Co-counseling the psychiatric patient with the medical professional is possible when the counselor's training includes adequate background in the psychopathological and psychological issues involved. Counselors may limit themselves to spiritual and supportive counseling with the psychiatric patient. Attempting to aid the family in maintaining communication, understanding the illness, coping, and finding courage during the devastation of a mental illness may be the counselor's most important task. It is one task the psychiatrist seldom has sufficient time to accomplish. The team concept works well in mental health clinics where physician time is difficult to get and most counseling is handled by mental health professionals who are not physicians.

Specific in-depth counseling of psychiatric illness is well beyond the scope of this text. The remainder of this chapter will deal with counseling the family to understand and cope with the devastation and stigma of mental illness and senility. It will also discuss the problems encountered with psychiatric medication.

## THE BIOCHEMICAL BRAIN

Mental illness in the time of Christ included epilepsy, palsy, and other neurologic conditions. It was generally viewed as "demon possession." Luke, a physician by training, describes the possession of a boy whose demon ". . . seizes him and he suddenly screams; it throws him into convulsions so that he foams at the mouth" (Luke 9:39 NIV). The paralytic whose sins were forgiven was also healed of his paralysis (Luke 5). And the Gadarene who was possessed by the "legion" of spirits was freed from his "lunatic" behavior of breaking chains, cutting himself, and living in tombs without clothing (Luke 8). The spirits in this man knew who Jesus was and knew his authority over them.

A strong case can be made for demon possession in some of the biblical accounts, just as it can be made in a few cases today (see Rodger Bufford's book on demon possession in the Resources for Christian Counseling series).[1] In biblical times, however, the cultural understanding of psychiatric disease consisted exclusively of demon possession. Today, many of these illnesses can be more appropriately explained in terms of biochemical deficiencies that alter mental function. Such deficiencies are found with the emotional and psychological components of psychiatric disease.

The human brain is a marvelous creation of cells that communicate by biochemical and electrical means. Charges pass along the surface of communicating *neurons* when ionic concentrations change. This ripple effect moves quickly and efficiently from one end of the cell to the other. At the *synapse,* where one cell communicates with another, biochemicals are released that will cause a charge to be produced in the next cell. The next cell then passes it along to the next, and so on.[2]

In the brain itself, there are billions of neurons. Many are specialized to perform specific functions, such as smell, vision, memory, emotions, movement, coordination, hearing, touch and others.[3] These cells gather information from thousands of other cells as the information is processed and a response generated.

Each of the functions of the brain can be decreased, altered or changed when biochemicals known as *neurohormones* are deficient or altered. These create problems with cell-to-cell communication. The emotional centers, personality areas, and coordination of senses and thoughts to form perceptions can be adversely affected through neurohormone deficiencies. Through intensive studies of the neurohormone levels in the brain tissues, and by knowing the actions of various psychiatric medications on the neurohormones, partially proven theories have been formulated about the causes of many psychiatric disorders.

The hypothesis that depression is caused by a reduction in one or more of these neurohormones is a well-accepted understanding by physicians and mental health professionals. Reduction in dopamine in the neurons of emotional areas, for example, leads to symptoms of depression.[4] Tri-cyclic antidepressants have been shown to increase dopamine levels, thus supporting the theory.

Other psychiatric medications work on other neurohormones in other areas of the brain.

Why do illegal drugs, alcohol and morphine alter the functioning of the brain? These biochemicals interact with the chemistry of the brain and alter neuron-to-neuron communication.[5] For example, chemicals such as LSD stimulate sensations, visions, or noises by changing electrical patterns within the brain.

How do emotions play a part in the origin or continuance of mental illness? Emotions are complex interactions between the senses, memories, and present thoughts. Serious emotional disturbances in the environment cause stress, which in turn changes the levels of neurohormones in the emotional centers of the brain. When these levels are lowered, the symptoms and emotions of depression may result. The lowered neurohormone levels may be the origin of altered emotions and physical symptoms and may self-perpetuate through the stress mechanism.[6]

## FUNCTION AND PSYCHIATRIC ILLNESS

Our present biochemical theories and the use of effective medications have changed the focus of psychiatric treatment from confinement to counseling and a return to normal function. The goal of any medication program is to help the individual become, as much as possible, a functioning member of society. Although the emphasis until the 1950s had been on confining those with "uncurable" mental diseases away from family and society, today even Freudian theories of mental illness have rapidly expanded to include the newer biochemical hypotheses.[7]

The medications discovered in the 1950s and 1960s helped empty our psychiatric facilities of all but the most intractable cases. Hospitalization was no longer permanent as long as effective therapy could be established. The stigma of mental illness began to fade as more and more people understood one of its causes—a chemical imbalance similar to diabetes or thyroid disease.

While some classes of patients were making advances, others were beginning to suffer in new ways. The burden of care for these difficult patients shifted, and the family has often been left with their guardianship. It has inherited all of the responsibilities and problems—from medication side effects to emotional outbursts, communication problems, financial burdens, and more. Making these patients function normally in our complex society is not always possible.

When physicians do not have time to help families cope with these "home care" issues for the psychiatrically ill, counselors, pastors and social workers are called to fill in. These professionals can add understanding, and remove a great deal of family guilt simply by being available and answering questions about the course of these chronic malfunctions.

The most important issue for the counselor and family to resolve is that of disease origin. A discussion of the family structure and communication patterns may reveal only minor problems that simple suggestions can settle. For many serious psychiatric disorders, no environmental causes may be found because the origin is biochemical. Knowing this often relieves guilt and allows the family to accept one member's illness as a "chance" situation. Helping family members accept responsibility for the outcome, and not the cause, will motivate them to assist in long-term care.

As Shandra's complicated case revealed, psychiatric disease is often accompanied by, or caused by, severe psychological changes that occur because of poor communication, marital dysfunction, learned behaviors from parents, and a host of other dysfunctional emotional states. These situations will need careful use of medications in combination with personal, family, and perhaps marital counseling. Again, whether or not the psychological dysfunction is caused by biochemical changes, the patient and family must concentrate on the treatment instead of laying blame on each other.

Denial of the situation—whether because of lack of understanding of psychiatric disease or lack of ability to cope with it—needs to be approached with as much guilt dissipation as possible. Some parents or siblings will still refuse to accept any responsibility for the ill patient, just as Shandra's parents did. They will try to push the counselor for more permanent hospitalization. The counselor may become squeezed between the family that doesn't want the patient home and the medical system that doesn't want him hospitalized. The only way to approach the family is through education and loving, supportive counseling. Hopefully, this will give members tools to form appropriate plans for dealing with the patient. The counselor may have to withdraw if the family refuses to accept responsibility or make reasonable decisions about the care of the psychiatrically ill person.

However, the counselor may become a consistent source of spiritual and emotional encouragement for the family that willingly takes responsibility for care of the "functioning" psychiatric patient. Functioning level varies greatly from person to person, from one diagnosis to another, and from the present to the future. As with all malfunctioning illnesses, changes are the rule, not the exception. An Alzheimer's patient may be functioning normally for a few days and then become confused and agitated overnight. A schizophrenic may be quiet and reclusive before the storm of blatant psychosis. The manic-depressive patient may be jubilant and happy and then, within a few days, may attempt suicide.

Medication will blunt the swings and, hopefully, prolong the periods of normal or near-normal functioning.

The family should be counseled to watch for warning signs that an individual's psychiatric problem is worsening: feeling depressed, hyperactivity, excessive phone calls, difficulty with simple tasks, and staring can all be symptomatic. The family offers the best environment for preventing exacerbations through open communication, loving and supportive gestures, and holding the patient accountable for any and all behavior. General spiritual encouragement is essential. As family members are tried and tested, they can be counseled to see God's love and purpose through mental illness.

## MEDICATION SIDE EFFECTS AND COUNSELING

It becomes inevitable that the professional counselor or pastor will deal with clients who are on medications, especially those prescribed to relieve anxiety and depression. Many of these patients are under the care of their family physician, not a psychiatrist. The number of patient encounters involving medication will require the counselor to have a working knowledge of some of the names of these medications, their common side effects, their desired effects, and how they should be taken. The counselor should never "practice medicine" by suggesting a change in the medication, stopping it, or increasing the dosage. To do so could incur severe liability. But knowing what a medication is supposed to do, and knowing its side effects, can help patient, family, and the prescribing physician. The counselor's observations may be helpful because patients often will not call their physician when having problems with medication.

Table 4 lists common medications, their generic and trade names, their common side effects, and their desired effects.

A physician's intent in prescribing a medication is always to help cure a problem or relieve suffering. But many medications have side effects which result in poor patient compliance or a poor patient result. They should be stopped, changed, or the dosage adjusted. Good communication with the prescribing physician can help in obtaining a good result for the patient. Ask patients if you can call and discuss their symptoms with their physicians. Follow up with the patients if you have suggested that they take responsibility to call. All physicians should answer a call about side effects of a medication within a few hours.

## CO-COUNSELING WITH A PHYSICIAN

Co-counseling patients can be a great benefit to all involved. Mental health clinics have used this model successfully for years, offering psychiatric medication prescribed by a physician, while maintaining most counseling needs through social workers

| Generic Name | Trade Name |
| --- | --- |

NEUROLEPTICS—used to reduce psychosis. Possible side effects include drowsiness, tiredness, uncoordination, and movement disorders.

- chlorpromazine — Thorazine
- fluphenazine — Prolixin
- haloperidol — Haldol
- loxapine — Loxitane
- mesoridazine — Serentil
- thiothixene — Navaron
- thioridazine — Mellaril
- trifluoperazine — Stelazine

ANTIDEPRESSANTS—used to reduce symptoms of depression. Possible side effects include drowsiness, tiredness, dry mouth.

- imipramine — Tofranil
- amitriptyline — Elavil
- desipramine — Norpramin
- maprotiline — Ludiomil
- doxepin — Adapin
- trazadone — Desyrel

TRANQUILIZERS—used to reduce the symptoms of anxiety or to induce sleep. Drowsiness or tiredness are the main side effects.

- chlordiazepoxide — Librium
- diazepam — Valium
- meprobamate — Equanil
- chlorazepate — Tranxene
- oxazepam — Serax
- orazepam — Verstran
- chloral hydrate — Noctec
- flurazepam — Dalmane
- pentobarbital sodium — Nembutal
- tamazepam — Restoril

STIMULANTS—used in attention-deficit disorders to stimulate attention and to control appetite. Side effects include anxiety, hyperactive behavior, and addiction.

- dl-amphetamine — Benzedrine
- d-amphetamine — Dexedrine
- pemoline — Cylert
- methylphenidate — Ritalin
- phenmetrazin — Preludin
- methamphetamine — Desoxyn

**Table 4**
**Psychiatric Medications: Use and Side Effects[8]**

or trained professional counselors. This extends the number of patients who can receive appropriate, therapeutic medication and desired counseling and support.

Almost everyone benefits from these co-counseling arrangements. The patient can keep medical costs down by needing only a brief office visit for medication adjustments or changes. The counselor continues to see his or her regular patients and maintains an established, trusting therapeutic relationship. The physician can see more patients and have fewer schedules interrupted by crisis counseling needs. The family also has better access to the counselor, who can help to repair damaged relationships and facilitate healing communication.

The basis for this counselor-patient-physician relationship needs to be communication and common goals. The physician and the counselor must communicate regularly about the patient, and a signed "information release" form should be kept by both. Common counseling goals should be maintained and discussed on a periodic basis. Any medications being given should be communicated to the counselor, who will be diligent to look for side effects. Passing letters is optimal for medico-legal reasons, but phone calls are often quicker and less costly.

The counselor needs to know his or her limitations and be willing to allow the counseling in some areas to be done by a professional if necessary. Consider, for example, a young woman who has been counseled for depression but suddenly admits to her counselor that she has had anorexia and bulimia. It is obvious that she has lost significant weight in the past few weeks and may be moving rapidly to a dangerous situation. Even though the counselor may be comfortable handling the depression, counseling and medication in a situation like this are often not enough. A strict inpatient program for eating disorders and referral to a psychiatrist and counseling staff that work with this problem full-time is the wisest choice. I have personally seen family physicians and counselors alike wait until the damage was almost irreversible. (For a full discussion on eating disorders, please refer to the Resources for Christian Counseling book on that topic.)[9] Timely referral and knowing one's own limitations are essential when counseling the psychiatrically ill.

Another excellent arrangement for counselors seeking to enlarge their practices is through the office of a physician group. The counselor can bring his or her established patients into the practice, and the association, in turn, brings ready access to new counseling patients referred from the group. The practice offers a source of billing for the counselor and possibly other insurance benefits as well. Many family physician groups have already taken this route by hiring part-time or full-time counseling help so they can concentrate on the science of medicine.

The major pitfalls with the co-counseling arrangement stem from personality conflicts, training differences and poor communication. Make sure you can talk freely and easily to the physicians with whom you work. Discuss how you would handle the general counseling in such areas as depression, anxiety, marital difficulties, and unresolved anger to see if your counseling styles are compatible. And, again, communicate often about progress and new issues to avoid duplication of counseling or the impression of "patient stealing."

## SENILITY

We were having a Bible study at our house one evening when an elderly gentleman shyly came up to the door. He stood still for about a minute, looking down at the porch and then back and forth between it and the door. Finally, he raised his hand and knocked.

He was a gentleman in his eighties who appeared to be confused. He could remember his name, but not where he lived. He believed that he was in Paris in the 1940s and had just finished fighting World War I. Questions about who he was and where he thought he was seemed to bounce off into space. He kept a slow, confused dialogue going with whomever he was looking at.

The daughter of this gentleman had telephoned the police, just as we had. Soon they were reunited. The daughter seemed rather cold to us and didn't want to talk about him or how he got to our house. She quickly and silently whisked him out of the front door without any acknowledgment of our offers to help.

The general aging of the population has dramatically increased the number of people diagnosed with senile dementia, whether through the normal aging process or prematurely through disease. A lack of nursing home space and high costs of care have forced many families to deal with their demented parent or spouse within their home. This can create stresses and emotional complications that counselors should understand. The counselor should also have a general awareness of the conditions of aging and their treatments.

Dementias can be broken down into two general classifications: senile dementia and presenile dementia.[10] Older adults who exhibit a slowly increasing loss of memory, apathy, and decreased comprehension fall into the first category. Adults in their fifties or sixties who take a rapidly progressive course toward senility are placed in the second classification. Temporary states of confusion that are reversed when the medical condition is improved, or the medication removed, are not classified as permanent dementias.[11]

Senile dementia is usually a slow, insidious disorder.

A dislike of change, a reduction in ambition and activity, a tendency to become constricted and self-centered in interests, increased difficulty in comprehension, increase in time and effort necessary for the performance of familiar duties, increasing difficulty in adapting to new circumstances, a lessened sympathy for new ideas and views, and a tendency to reminiscence and repetition are scarcely signs of senile dementia, yet they (these mild signs of dementia) pass imperceptibly into mental destitution and personality regression.[12]

Anxiety, depression, irritability, and other emotional symptoms may overlay the deficiencies in memory and function. These may need medical treatment as well as involvement in counseling therapy.

Alzheimer's disease is the most serious of the presenile dementias. Other members of the family may become afflicted with this disorder as they grow older. The symptoms for Alzheimer's patients are similar to all senile states: a slow, progressive impairment in cognitive function progresses to deficits in memory, judgment, orientation, and general reality. After a few years of progressing mental losses, the patient rapidly degenerates to the point of death. Seizures, spastic extremities, incontinence and a total lack of speech or recognition may be evidence of the final stages leading to a premature death.[13] Diagnosis can be made at autopsy and may be confirmed prior to death by family history, computerized axial tomography, biopsies and nuclear magnetic resonance scanning.

Therapy for those with senility is primarily supportive family care in a protected, organized environment. Specific medications to slow the progression, or to cure the process, are still experimental. No promising medications are on the horizon. Tranquilizers may reduce the confusion seen in these patients. Loving family support is still the best, most effective non-medical treatment.

## Family Support in Dementia

The counselor may become involved with a patient in the early stages of senility because of changes in personality, decreases in memory, or emotional symptoms. He or she should encourage the patient to seek medical attention when senility is just beginning. Correctable causes may be discovered, such as medication side effects or a brain mass. Once a proper diagnosis is established, general spiritual and emotional supportive counseling can begin. This includes educating patients about the progressive, degenerative changes of dementia, helping them accept and deal with the consequences of the disease, and preparing the family for the slow downhill course, including death.

Family members will receive most of the counseling. Their frustration, anger, and guilt may build to intolerable levels as their family member exhibits bizarre, unpredictable behavior. A patient may go to bed apparently normal and wake up at 4 A.M. to walk the streets without any clothing. He or she may be unable to differentiate among different foods and ask repeatedly about a person or a situation. Strong emotional outbursts are common.

Supportive counseling for the family can be the outlet needed to forestall these brewing emotions before they turn into abusive or neglectful attitudes toward senile parents. Support groups are available in many larger and some smaller cities for those whose parents or spouses have Alzheimer's disease.[14]

# CHAPTER EIGHT

## COUNSELING THE TERMINALLY ILL

During an individual's lifetime, often nothing causes more fear or more distress than anticipating the pain and suffering associated with death. What people dread most is physical pain—whether sharp, dull, constant, gnawing, searing, or knife-like. Many also fear dying alone and some fear the emotional pain of separation, of seeing a loved one suffer, or of having to let go.

Our materialistic society values youth, energy, vitality, good health, and enjoyment, but it sees little use in growing old. It spoils our lustful image of life. We are so addicted to life's pleasures—to feeling good—that we have forgotten the need to grow through trials, to mature through testing, to "graduate" to eternal life with our Savior.

Many books have tried to explain emotional reactions to death in individuals or in families. They observe the human defense mechanisms easing the dying patient into an understanding and acceptance of the inevitable. It is a normal human response to feel remorse about leaving behind loved ones and cherished possessions.[1] But seeing the death of a few mature Christians has changed my mind about our ideal counsel for the dying and the terminally ill.

Martha was eighty-two-years old and lay dying of colon cancer, her liver almost completely filled with cancerous metastases. Although she was in pain, she had a calmness, peace, and joy that seemed impossible for someone in her physical condition.

I had the privilege of talking with her and receiving counsel from her two days before her death.

"How have you dealt with knowing that you were soon to die?" I asked.

"I have always known that I was going to die, ever since I was saved," she said. "I have always looked forward to dying, not because of what I am leaving, but because of what I am gaining."

"At first, didn't you go through a phase of denial, of bargaining or of disbelief?"

"How could I deny what I was looking forward to. How could I bargain with a God who is perfect and holy. I have nothing to bargain with. Why should I disbelieve what God said was necessary—the trials and testings of life. I was ready to let go long before I was asked."

"The cancer is obviously causing some pain. Why are you not taking any pain medication?" I asked.

"God is proving His love for me," Martha responded. "He told me that trials were to help me grow. I want to keep growing and maturing until this body no longer has breath."

My next question embarrassed her. "Are you following Christ's example when he refused the wine mixed with gall from the cross?"

Her face turned red as she answered, "I am not worthy to be likened unto him. But I know why he didn't take it. He knew the pain would keep him alert so he could be praying for you and for me. That's what I try to do. I keep my mind off the pain by praying for the needs of my family."

"Are you concerned about suffering during the moments near death?" I quietly asked.

"With my eyes on him, he has promised me the strength to go through any suffering. He already has given me the strength to go through what I have now."

She was waiting to die. She was already dead in Christ and alive in him. Her transition from the mortal to the immortal happened two days later, as peacefully as a dream.

Dealing with patients can sometimes be an exceptional education for the counselor. Before Martha, I had always thought of death as a positive change, but I had seen few Christians actually fulfill this ideal. The counselor is seldom called for the mature and the ready, however. He or she must help those who handle death's process with confusion, anger, despair, and frustration, and help comfort their families in bereavement.

The entire process of terminal illness can be briefly considered from a clinical perspective, looking at physical and emotional processes involved. A suggested reading list of other books that will give the reader a more detailed psychodynamic approach to counseling the terminally ill is included at the end of this book.

## LIFE EXPECTANCY, PROGNOSIS, AND TERMINAL ILLNESS

The physician has just entered the room and somberly told his patient "We've got to talk." She has been in the hospital for three days having x-rays and blood taken. They even put her in the "big doughnut" or CT scanner. The pain in the pit of her stomach had grown worse for about two months, and the nausea was so bad she had expected something serious.

"After all the testing, we have discovered a mass in your pancreas," the physician tells her. "This appears to be a large, tumorous mass that has spread to your liver and the surrounding tissues. We think that it is pancreatic cancer."

All she hears is "CANCER—CANCER—CANCER" echoing

in her mind. But in her heart she knew it was! All that weight loss. It just made sense.

"Doctor, how long do I have to live?" she asks.

"It is so advanced that there is little to no chance of a cure. Even with aggressive surgery, it is only likely to give you a few more weeks. You probably have between two weeks and three months to live."

"Is there any chance you are wrong about the disease?"

The physician just lowers his head and shakes it. "No."

Most patients are well aware of the seriousness of their medical problem before they receive bad news from a physician. They have lived with their bodies long enough to know the signs of a serious versus a minor disorder. Few are truly surprised except the young patient diagnosed with a rare fatal illness.

Mature Christians may be granted by the Lord the knowledge that their time to die is imminent. Dr. B. R. Lakin told his wife before they climbed on the plane that this was his last trip to Lynchburg, Va. He just seemed to know he was going to die there. He preached an excellent sermon that Sunday, but he fell ill two days later and needed to be hospitalized. Though the original reason for his treatment was improving, early one morning he died quickly and painlessly from a heart attack.

His premonition was correct. I have known of a number of Christians who were granted the same privilege. Some non-Christians have said the same about their deaths.

In fact, the patient's understanding of death's imminence is often more correct than the physician's, and herein lies the problem of prognosis and death expectancies. A given disease is so variable, and a given individual so different from others, that an accurate "you will die this week" is often impossible. About 5 to 20 percent of these patients will die earlier than expected, possibly because they have given up and resigned themselves to death. About 70 percent will succumb to their disease in the time frame predicted. A small percentage, about 5 percent will outlive their death expectancy. Some live longer because they are too stubborn to die. Others have too much to live for. Some outlive the prognosis because of a wrong diagnosis.

Approximately 1 percent of serious diseases will spontaneously resolve themselves without any medical treatment.

We have all heard of "miraculous" situations: the mother who, though diagnosed with ovarian cancer and given just a few weeks to live, ends up living two years until both of her daughters are married; the father whose lung cancer never kills him, but instead continues to grow smaller and smaller. These could be either God's direct intervention or rare, spontaneous remissions.

We have two reasons to offer hope and encouragement to the patient no matter what the prognosis, disease outcome, or range of death expectancy. First, hope can always be drawn from the statistics that a spontaneous cure may occur even if the chance is very small. Second, positive expectations about the outcome will improve the longevity of the patient simply because hope-filled encouragement has positive therapeutic benefit for dying patients.

Patients who have just been told that life is quickly ending often suffer a shock-like reaction. Their thinking is clouded and their thoughts become fixed on single words or phrases. They may not remember who was in the room when they heard the diagnosis, what was talked about or any information about the disease. Many physicians know this is likely to occur so they give the report, then wait until the next day to fill in the details of expectancies, treatments, or outcomes. This is not the time to force the patient into making decisions. It is also not the time to begin positive outcome discussions—the patient will look at you and say, "Didn't you hear that I was going to die?"

Listen to patients during this initial shock stage, allowing them to talk through the disbelief, shock, and denial. Letting patients talk through their defenses speeds the return to clear thinking. Our patients then need to absorb the next layer of information, the disease specifics and treatment options. This is where the ministry of counseling the dying patient begins. Your expertise in guiding them through the medical maze, digesting and simplifying medical information, and soothing their emotional reactions as they enter the first stage of the grief process will be well received.

Some patients start the early stages of the grief process before they learn their diagnosis. They often deny that theirs is a serious or life-threatening problem. They may begin to bargain with God, offering service and allegiance in exchange for a good diagnosis. Anxiety, restlessness, and fear are commonly present before the diagnosis, and as it sinks in, the emotional reactions will be intense. Patients may experience waves of grief and return to denial, confusion, or repeated feelings of numbing shock.

Whatever physical signs and emotions precede or accompany the diagnosis, the grieving process must be started unless immediate illness claims the patient first. The fear of death, and the fear of losing emotional control, are two major reasons many people pray to die quickly.

## GRIEVING AND COUNSELING

Grief is a multi-staged, somewhat organized, very individual process. As we saw in chapter 1, many have attempted to bring some order to the understanding of the grief reaction. Worden suggests four major tasks—acceptance, pain experiencing, readjustment, and re-relationship.[2] Hodge suggests the following stages must occur (but not necessarily in order): shock and surprise, emotional release, loneliness, anxiety and physical distress, panic, guilt, hostility and projection, suffering silence, gradual overcoming, and readjustment. Parkes uses these four stages: (1) numbness, shock and denial, (2) yearning for the loss, (3) disorganization and despair, and (4) reorganization.[3]

Contemplation of death, grieving for the loss of a loved one, and the psychological process of dealing with illness are virtually identical and contain similar stages and elements. The healthy response to these human events must include an understanding of the process, an acceptance of the outcome, and a recovery or readjustment phase for rebuilding self-esteem and relationships. The contrasting unhealthy response to grief may never get started; but when it does, it is characterized by persistent denial of reality. Anger, frustration, guilt and despair smother cognitive understanding and acceptance of the disease. Suppression, regression, substitution, and many other defenses cause the patient to substitute abnormal new relationships that further hamper the grieving process.

As suggested in the first chapter, we can construct a more workable grief model that fulfills both the secular and Christian understanding of the dying patient and his or her emotional needs. We have used the term Unified Theory of Grief to describe a three-stage grieving process (reaction, acceptance, growth) seen in those suffering from a temporary illness or living the final stage of life. Secular psychologists have adequately described the first two phases of grief. But they have fallen short in describing the final one—spiritual and emotional growth. This, however, is the ultimate purpose of suffering. The cascade of emotional reaction to acceptance and growth is the same whether the individual is grieving for suffering or grieving for sin. Not only does sickness and grief expose one's physical vulnerability and mortality, but it highlights the same emotional needs that often lead to a spiritual decision for conversion.

Scripture strongly supports the observation that grieving brings forth spiritual fruit. The prophet Isaiah suggests that the Lord will reward and soothe those that grieve, and grow them into trees that will glorify him:

> To appoint unto them that mourn in Zion, to give unto them beauty for ashes, the oil of joy for mourning, the garment of praise for the spirit of heaviness; that they might be called trees of righteousness, the planting of the Lord, that he might be glorified. (Isa. 61:3)

In 2 Timothy 2:1–13, Paul admonishes young Timothy to "endure hardness as a good soldier of Jesus Christ." He states suffering is essential if we are to reign with him.

In Hebrews 12, Paul suggests that God's chastening—whether through beatings, hunger, scourgings, loneliness, or persecution—is for our profit:

> that we might be partakers of His holiness. Now no chastening for the present seemeth to be joyous, but grievous:

146

nevertheless afterward it yieldeth the peaceable fruit of righteousness unto them which are exercised thereby.

(Heb. 12:10, 11)

James also suggests the high calling of grief.

Be afflicted, and mourn, and weep: let your laughter be turned to mourning, and your joy to heaviness. Humble yourselves in the sight of the Lord, and he shall lift you up.

(James 4:9, 10)

Other Scriptures link mourning of sin to forgiveness. Grieving leads to cleansing, to righteousness, to salvation, to a closer relationship with God.

The counselor can, and should, counsel patients to see these three steps of grieving that have been simplified into the Unified Theory. But counseling is incomplete if it does not teach patients the purpose of grieving, that God has lovingly allowed sickness, disease, and death to restore our rebellious generation. If they can see grief in its spiritual simplicity, they are more likely to grow through its testing.

I personally cannot believe a loving God would allow pain and suffering to continue in his creation if he had not assigned an extremely important purpose to it: to reclaim the rebellious, to bring many to God, and to mature the saints. Even the suffering of Christ was permitted because of the great spiritual harvest that it realized.

## Pathological Grief

Unfortunately, most patients will not handle the grieving process as Martha did. A few will quickly work through their emotional reactions and accept the present situation. More will reach the acceptance phase slowly, through much questioning and emotional turmoil. Others will become deeply entrenched in the emotional reaction phase, never willing to let go of bitterness, anger, and resentment, never willing to accept loss. This persistent reaction to grief with dysfunctional emotions and thoughts is termed "pathological grief" and will need to be dealt with in the counseling office.

147

Counseling the patient to initiate the grieving process is the most difficult step when dealing with delayed, morbid, or pathological grief.[4] The suddenness of the death and the shock-like reaction appear to be major factors blocking the start of grieving.[5] Denial of the situation, paralyzed emotions, and lack of decision-making capabilities never allow the family member to start grieving during the visitation, the services or the burial. Amnesia of much of that time has been reported by widows—obviously a defense mechanism to forget the emotional pain experienced. Excessive dependence upon the victim, whether dying or dead, does not allow the loved one to give up his or her denial. Regression, and transference of dependence to the counselor, pastor, surviving family, or other support system is also common. All, if excessive, may be symptoms of unhealthy grief.[6]

Other factors that may influence the ability of the family to grieve are numerous. The role the dead member occupied is an important determinant of the depth of the emotional response.[7] Each member's coping behaviors, personality structure and present mental health will also determine the grief reaction, and the member's past experiences with loss or death are often an indicator of the grief reaction's course. Other social, ethnic, and cultural factors also play a role.[8]

When attempting to diagnose the abnormal grief process, probe for the issues that play a role in the blockage. What were the relationship characteristics between the patient and the deceased? In what ways was the patient dependent, and in what ways was the deceased dependent? How much guilt about negative situations is present? Was the death preventable, untimely, sudden, or unexpected? Was the patient allowed by the deceased to grieve in his or her presence before death occurred? What other secondary losses (the loss of income, for example) have been sustained? If the loved one is still dying, how is he or she handling the pain, the treatments and the self-grieving process?[9]

Dealing with unhealthy grief requires an organized plan, something like the "care plan" previously described, to help a counselee through the difficult complications of his or her own emotional reactions and their causes. An orderly, step-by-step plan, based upon the Worden grief therapy process, will help you to deal with pathological grief in those you counsel.

The following guidelines are for dealing with prolonged, delayed, or excessive grief reactions.[10]

1. Rule out any physical cause for the symptoms if the grief reaction is violent or excessive.
2. Begin the counseling process by examining the relationships and losses that the grieving person has sustained. Always put these losses in the context of God's eternal purpose for suffering and grief to bring maturity.
3. Openly talk about the dying process, the death itself, and memories of the deceased. Deal with each loss as it is revived.
4. Discuss each loss in terms of acceptance. Discuss the changes the loss will require in the person's life.
5. Deal with the appropriateness of emotions stimulated by the memories and give permission to emotionally grieve. Ask the patient to put aside symbols of the deceased and substitute memories only after a final acceptance has been achieved.
6. Counsel the patient to set goals for his or her new life— new dreams, new visions, new ministries—to begin the growth phase of grieving.
7. Continue a counseling relationship until the patient can verbalize an acceptance of all the losses, begin to achieve some of the objectives and goals discussed, and verbalize how God has used these situations to help further understand the spiritual principles of maturity.

The counselor must also consider the dying patient. Even though many psychologists have described variations and used different terminology, virtually no differences exist between the grief process of the dying patient and that of his or her family. The dying patient may suffer from a grief that is further amplified by the physical suffering he or she is experiencing. But the patient must understand the physical and psychological processes that have led to this terminal illness, accept its presence and readjust to the plight. Counseling of these patients must take into account their physical discomfort, their increased sense of urgency, and their impressions of support from family and others.

### The Physical Response to Grief

On most stress scales, personal illness, illness of a spouse, or death of a spouse rank among the greatest stresses possible during a human lifetime. The neurologic effects of stress on the autonomic nervous system create excessive stimulation of the stomach, intestines, blood pressure, and heart rate. The process produces symptoms of anxiety and releases the adrenaline hormone. Adrenaline also stimulates the same organs, giving the patient a double overdose of stress. The autonomic stimulation leads to such physical symptoms as increased heart rate and force, chest tightness, hyperventilation, clammy skin, inability to relax or sleep, increased stomach acidity, hypermotility, diarrhea, and shaking.

Stress has been shown in numerous studies to decrease the defenses of the body's immune system and increase the possibility of infection.[11] Any diseases already present—skin conditions, ulcers, thyroid problems, diabetes, bowel problems—are all made worse during immune system compromise. The body's metabolic balance is thrown off, causing tiredness, weakness, apathy, and sleep problems.

All of these problems and symptoms depend upon the individual's response to the grieving process. A person who quickly and easily grieves for the expected loss of a parent will experience few, if any, symptoms. The overly dependent individual who suddenly loses a spouse in a catastrophic accident and persists in the shock stage of pre-grief will have the hardest time with stress and sickness.

Are these symptoms only in the mind of the griever? Absolutely not! These are real results, from real feelings, which lead to real health problems. Never let patients believe a physician when he or she says, "These problems are just in your head." The symptoms may be generated or perpetuated by psychological factors, but they are still real physical pains, aches, and problems. Many of these physical symptoms resolve spontaneously when grieving is finished, but this may take weeks or months.

## DEALING WITH THE FEAR OF
## PAIN IN DEATH

One fear—that of painful death—has created more pathological grief reactions than all the others.

Pain and suffering do accompany many terminal illnesses, but the attitude that the patient holds toward this pain controls whether it is tolerable or intolerable. A number of the Christian patients that I have attended with chronic or near-death pain have exemplified this principle. Those who remain bitter toward God for their disease routinely have more pain problems and require more medication; those who accept the disease and look forward to their eventual homegoing do not complain as much. When asked about their pain, those who accept disease often suggest the suffering is present, but tolerable.

Although many people fear that passing from life to death is painful, experience contradicts them. Almost all patients who have experienced a near-death situation (the patient was clinically dead except for extraordinary life-support) suggest it was a peaceful experience. Others describe a calm floating, gentle breezes, and effortless gliding.[12] A dear friend of our family had to be revived when she stopped breathing and her heart stopped. Annie describes the most peaceful, joy-filled place that can be imagined. She had difficulty finding words to describe the exhilaration of this experience.

But Annie is a wonderful Christian lady, and the fear of pain in death has obvious spiritual significance. It is an innate fear, a God-instilled fear designed to draw us to him. The few negative accounts of near-death experiences all seem to describe a hellish place. Burning, pain, emptiness, intense loneliness, indescribable darkness are the characteristics of some of these experiences. The fear of pain in death seems an appropriate response to our fear of judgment and banishment in hell.

### Pain Medication in Terminal Illness

Our medical system has accomplished one feat very well, that of suppressing or removing pain. We have a great armamentarium to relieve pain—general anesthesia, injectible medications, and pills. If we cannot cure the problem, at least we can cure its painful consequences.

Giving pain relief indiscriminately has brought many social and personal problems. Addiction to these medications and an uncontrollable seeking for stronger illegal pain relievers and euphorics are at an all-time high. The cost of these medications (within the context of our entire health care budget) is in the billions of dollars. People today expect to be pain-free at all times, and the least headache or injury must be eliminated by medication, even though the problem would otherwise correct itself naturally.

Of major concern is the appropriateness of relieving pain in the dying patient. Should the patient choose when to get pain medication and in what amount? Do patients have sufficiently full mental capabilities to continue the grieving process? Are patients still responsive to family and visitors? Do some medications help the short-term pain, but prolong life and suffering?

If our patients are suffering, and we have the means to relieve that suffering, it should be their right to obtain relief if they so desire. Physicians often write medication orders for their own convenience. As long as the patient needs the medicine for relief and receives it at a level that keeps drowsy side effects tolerable, then the painkiller is appropriate.

But consider the ethical, emotional, and spiritual problems in the situation where a terminal patient is kept so drugged that he cannot respond to his family. He never regains mental faculties because injections are given every four hours whether needed for pain relief or not. This patient no longer can make his own decisions. He is unable to be involved in the grief process and its benefits. If he has been unable to handle the grieving process, shot after shot will not help to deal with emotional reactions or accept dying. Spiritually, this patient has not been allowed to grow through testings or to come to salvation on his deathbed.

In most situations, physicians are not sure how death is either hastened or prolonged. A strong possibility exists that extended pain relief may actually prolong the life of the patient. Stress mechanisms are kept at a lower level and the emotions are, too.

When Jesus was nailed to the cross and hung there dying, he was offered a potion that would have relieved some of his pain. But it also would have suppressed his respirations, decreased his strength, perhaps clouded his mind, and hastened his death.

Christ's death was a purposeful one: He died for the sins of all men. If he had taken the medication, critics could have said "See, he wasn't God because he couldn't take the pain." If his respirations had been suppressed, people might not have been able to hear his words. Since most died on the cross from asphyxiation, he could have died before he stated "It is finished." If his mind had been clouded, he might have said the wrong thing.

For Jesus, pain medication was a temptation to be avoided.

Thankfully, our deaths will not be for another's salvation. But our witness through our death may be diminished. God's purpose of testing through disease and pain may be negated. Our minds may be so clouded that we will hurt our loved ones with confused words or a lack of attention.

Counseling the dying patient can be much more fruitful if all aspects of care and death work together to bring physical, emotional, and spiritual comfort to the patient and family.

## THE IDEAL COUNSEL FOR THE DYING

Praise the Lord from the earth, you great sea creatures and all ocean depths, lightning and hail, snow and clouds, stormy winds that do his bidding, you mountains and hills, fruit trees and all cedars, wild animals and all cattle, small creatures and flying birds, kings of the earth and all nations, you princes and all rulers of the earth, young men and maidens, old men and children. Let them praise the name of the Lord.                    (Ps. 148:7–13)

God has called all creation to "praise his holy name." For those who desire to serve him with thankful hearts, everything that we say or do should and can bring praise to him—including pain, sickness, suffering, dying, death, and grief.

I believe that it is possible to use this thought when we counsel the dying patient or families in grief. Do we dwell in our counseling time on dealing with the losses, or can we stress the gains that have been made, including spiritual gains? Do we reinforce negative images of death, pain, separation, and hopelessness by using secular psychological formulas for grief counseling? Shouldn't we be reinforcing the positive aspects of death: the joy, the peace, the probability of minimal or no pain, the permanent fellowship with our Savior? People can be a glorious witness for Christ on their deathbeds as they long for the moment when they will be with him.

I will forever be grateful to my patient Martha, who so completely changed my secular medical view of the "defeat of death" into the spiritual victory of death. "O, death, where is thy sting; O, grave, where is thy victory?" (1 Cor. 15:55). Long before Martha died, she had finished the grieving process. She already had "nine toes in heaven."

Not all Christians will approach death with the joy that Martha must have experienced. But God can use us—as physicians, as counselors, as pastors, as friends, or as family—to encourage our dying brother or sister in Christ to accept the beauty of suffering, the joy of pain, the maturation of death. We cannot judge when the patient is unable to grasp and live these spiritually mature concepts, but we can encourage.

Even through death we can praise our Creator, just as Martha has done.

## PART THREE

# MINISTRY IN TIMES
# OF SICKNESS

# CHAPTER NINE

# SPECIAL MEDICAL SITUATIONS

Phil's father, who had been divorced for a number of years, was in the middle of an extended visit. Currently suffering from severe rheumatoid arthritis, he had sustained two heart attacks and had lung problems from many years of smoking. All at the ripe old age of fifty-eight. And now he lay on the floor grasping his chest and crying "This is it!"

Phil had never used cardiopulmonary resuscitation (CPR) before, but he started in as his wife called the rescue squad. In a few minutes, the men arrived and took over. They quickly placed an endotracheal breathing tube and continued the chest compressions. Within thirty minutes, his heart started again, but there were no other signs of life.

After transport to the hospital, Phil's father was put in the cardiac intensive care unit and placed on a respirator. His heart rate was monitored, and his fluid status and vital signs were checked often. When his nervous system remained inactive, brain tests were ordered. These showed the presence of very few brain waves. Otherwise, his condition did not change for a week despite the physician's suggestion that death was likely at any moment.

The pressure to make a decision kept mounting: Should Phil heed the doctor's advice and remove his father from the breathing machine? He would die in fifteen minutes. Was his father's answer, "Yeah, I believe that stuff," a real profession of faith or a means of getting Phil off his back? Was there any hope for recovery? Shouldn't Phil let him die because he had suffered enough from his other diseases?

Phil had only one piece of advice from his father to help guide the decision: "I sure hope I die of a heart attack. It's usually so swift." His father had received half of his wish.

After much prayer, Phil felt at peace about the decision to take his father off the machines, but he decided to sleep on it and let the Lord confirm that decision. When Phil arrived at the hospital in the morning the physician said that the father's condition had worsened. He would die if other medication were not started. That was enough of a confirming sign for Phil.

His father died five minutes after the physician turned off the respirator.

Most of us look at this case and pray that we will not be put in the difficult place of having to make life-or-death decisions for our loved ones. But the miracles of modern medical technology make the prolongation of life increasingly possible and Phil's predicament will confront many people. Synthetic parts and pieces of the human body, as they become more plentiful, will allow physicians to replace worn-out parts and prolong life. Medications and support systems will allow greater function, less pain, and longer life in spite of impairments or handicaps.

Interestingly, the increased use of these technologies has fostered a large group of people who despise them. Many are writing wills to sue the physician who puts them on life support.

They refuse to have their natural functions prolonged by unnatural means. This knee-jerk reaction unfortunately burns valuable bridges for helping them with a correctable medical problem.

What are the correct, the scriptural, the humane answers to these questions and issues about prolonging life?

Books have been and will be written about these topics, but they are filled with secular and relativistic perspectives. A need for answers to these difficult questions will always be with us, and we will have to expand and clarify them as technology changes.

In this chapter, we will deal with the topics of medically necessary abortion, euthanasia, life-prolonging procedures, and suicide. We will look at each from a scriptural, a practical, and a common-sense approach. First, let's outline some basic principles that will apply to the decision-making process and to the outcome of all of these situations.

## PRINCIPLES FOR DECISION-MAKING

In a life-or-death decision, the patient should always be the one to make the decision, whether he or she wants to or not. This has been a time-honored ethic that hopefully will continue. Families should fulfill the wishes of the ill member to the best of their ability and the ability of our medical system.

But if the person is obviously confused, the spouse or family must sort through their recollections of the patient's previous desires and make the decision. Scripture is clear that personal decisions—decisions of behavior, thoughts, feelings—and their consequences fall on each of us, and God holds each of us responsible for them (Eph. 4:17–32; Gal. 5:16–26).

When a patient is mentally incapacitated, the spouse is the next person to make decisions because of the legalities of the marital contract. Spiritually, God has joined the marriage partners into one loving unit (Gen. 2:24) and no other person is as likely to make a correct, loving decision for a dying mate. But be wary of allowing separated or previous spouses to help make a decision for their dying mates. It may not be legal, nor is it spiritually advised.

The family is next if the spouse cannot make a treatment,

159

care, or termination decision. The commandment, "Honor thy father and mother" (Ex. 20:12) suggests that family members are charged with the responsible action of bringing praise to their parents. Making the best, most responsible, most caring decision will bring great honor and comfort to a dying parent.

When the patient, spouse, or family is unable to make a decision, the next in line should be the physician, then the court. The physician should always have the patient's best medical interest in mind. Hopefully, he or she has developed a caring relationship with the patient. But beware of this option. Many physicians today are biased toward letting an older patient go because of the high costs of medical care. The court has a legal responsibility to make an informed, caring decision for the patient when everyone else declines. The court may also be called upon to judge between the family and physician when they are at odds and the patient is unable to decide. The trend in U.S. courts is to line up with the "withdraw care quickly" side because of the societal costs of medical care.

It should be noted that the counselor and pastor have no legal, ethical, moral, or spiritual right to make a life-or-death decision for a patient. Their purpose and right is to help patients make the best, most informed, and most spiritually sensitive decision.

It is essential that patients communicate their desires about such matters as funerals and life-prolonging care to their spouse, family, and physician. One of three different means may be used while the patient is still well enough to make decisions. A living will gives patients opportunity to express their desires about prolonging life or receiving extraordinary care, and it has the power of law. A durable power of attorney is not as inflexible as the living will in the "gray" areas of medical decisions, but it relies upon another person to make life-and-death decisions for the patient.[1]

For the one who feels uncomfortable with either the durable power of attorney or the living will, a third intermediate method is possible. Patients may write down a list of wishes and desires to help guide—but not force—decision making if they become unable to make their own decisions. Figure 6 is a simple form letter and can be copied and given to spouses, children, distant family members and the family physician.

Dear family and physician:

In the event that I should become unable to make medical care decisions for myself, please use the following to help guide your decisions in caring for me:

1. If the accident, illness or event has left me with no mental abilities, please care for my body as if caring for a child—I would desire food, water, and medical care.

2. If the accident, illness or event has left me unconscious, supported only by machines, and with little hope of recovery, my desire would be to be removed from the machines after all hope for recovery is gone or after a few days of no electrical brain activity.

3. In the event of a prolonged illness that renders me unable to make care decisions for myself, please provide medical comfort, medication, food, and water for me. If the illness is terminal, please do not use extraordinary means of life support or resuscitation such as CPR, or breathing machines.

4. In the event of my death, please embalm and bury me in the family plot (already purchased) on _____ Street, in the burial vault (already purchased) at _____ Burial Supply.

Please remember that these are desires only. This is not a legal document. I realize that situations are almost never black and white, and I will trust my spouse, my family, or my physician to use their best judgment in deciding my medical care if I am unable. I make these desires known to you because of my love for you, and my love for the Lord Jesus Christ, with whom I will be living in the event of my bodily death.

I am willing to give up this body as I have already made my eternal decision, to trust the Lord Jesus as my Savior and to be born again (John 3). It is my desire to spend eternity with you as well, and I hope that you will trust Christ as your Savior, too. Please give me a call, or drop me a note, or read the enclosed tract so that you can know how to have eternal life.

Sincerely,

**Figure 6**
**Personal Medical Care Decisions Letter[2]**

This specific document can be tailored to fit individual needs, desires, beliefs, and family wishes. It should be emphasized that this is not a legal document that would bind family members or penalize them if they are unable to follow it, and it should not be seen as a living will that has legal implications for medical care. It is simply a means of solid, retrievable communication between the patient, the family, and the physician. As may be seen from the last paragraph, it could also become a tool to evangelize an unbelieving physician or family member.

## MAKING DECISIONS FOR OTHERS

When making a life-or-death decision for a loved one, it is essential that the family members reach orderly, prioritized, logical choices instead of ones based on emotions. They will need help in collecting resources that are available and they may want to discuss these decisions with a counselor before they make a mistake.

The utmost priority should be spiritual regeneration.[3] If the patient is a believer, any painful, life-prolonging procedures may mean prolonged separation from eternal joy. The other side of the coin is obvious: If the person is an unbeliever, prolonging life becomes more important to allow the patient to avoid eternal separation from God. This prolongation should be humane, not excessive, and it should fit within the spouse's or family's desires. But when the family is not sure whether to prolong, and the patient has not made a profession of faith, we can counsel them to "comfortably sustain" the patient while offering every opportunity to believe.

Does this mean we should dogmatically counsel families to turn off machines if the person has come to faith, and prolong life if he or she has not? Humane comfort should always be a primary issue. After salvation, the possibility of full physical recovery, full mental recovery, and the level of pain are the next priorities.

Our study of this issue is given little help from secular sources, whose criteria for prolonging life are based on "personhood," "quality of life," or long-term mental function.[4] Many others cited in the bibliography at the end of this book have discussed these issues from a religious perspective. They offer ideas ranging from a liberal—almost secular—slant to a conservative view of scripture and the sanctity of life. Many seem more intended for scholarly review than for helping patients make these difficult decisions.

Figure 7 is a prioritized list of pros and cons that we can use to help families make these difficult health decisions. It is a

|  | PRO | CON |
|---|---|---|
| **1. *Salvation*** | | |
| Is the patient born again? | yes | no |
| (If the answer is no, can we give him or her another chance to decide for Christ while comfortably prolonging life?) | | |
| **2. *Age*** | | |
| Has the patient lived a long, full, and productive life? | yes | no |
| **3. *Medical Condition*** | | |
| Is the medical condition terminal? | yes | no |
| Are there other medical problems that will shorten life or prolong suffering? | yes | no |
| Will the patient have little ability to think, or be in a vegetative state? | yes | no |
| Will use of "heroic treatments" or life support be extremely uncomfortable? | yes | no |
| **4. *Emotional Situation*** | | |
| Has the patient been able to grieve over the long-term illness? | yes | no |
| Has he or she accepted the situation? | yes | no |
| Did he or she express that all major personal issues have been finished? | yes | no |
| **5. *Personal Questions*** | | |
| Will prolonging the life of the patient cause great emotional, familial, or financial hardship on the spouse or children? | yes | no |
| Is it likely that extensive, costly care will be necessary for months or years, and that there is no means of paying for that care except through complete financial sacrifice of the family? | yes | no |

Circle every answer that pertains to the patient's situation. Please notice that the list provides no score and no formula. These are simply questions to help you consider logically some matters that should be decided before withdrawing life-prolonging treatment. The more "yes" answers circled, the more comfortable you should feel in making a decision to withdraw extraordinary treatments.

**Figure 7
Assessing Health Decisions[5]**

systematic way to place the patient's spiritual need first and look logically at all the options.

As previously discussed, the compassion-sacrifice-obedience decision pathway may also be useful. All decisions for terminally ill family members must be filled with as much compassion as possible. If a number of situations are all equally compassionate, the decision that involves the most personal sacrifice for the survivors often glorifies God the most. Any medical care decision should also be based, as best we are able, on obedience to scriptural principles and scriptural examples.

Let's apply the above principles to Phil's father's situation.

Who was the decision maker? Phil was the closest family member because his father was without a spouse. The decision should have been discussed between Phil and any other children.

On the list of priorities, the major question was that of salvation. Phil took every opportunity to speak with his father about his soul while his father was suspended on life support. Even though his father did not respond, Phil was still faithful to give him the plan of salvation repeatedly as if he could hear and respond. Phil's father's age was under sixty, but his condition was terminal. His complicating medical situations were serious. The pain of these problems was intense, and his father was likely to have little or no mental faculties if he were to survive. In the con column were most of the other options (grieving, unfinished business, and personal questions).

Because of the pain and suffering, the compassionate choice seemed to be to withdraw the respirator. At this point, it was no more sacrificial for Phil to suggest continuing on the machines or withdrawing from them. In obedience to scripture, it would be wise to continue until Phil was sure of his father's salvation. Since Phil made every effort possible, he was obedient.

There is never a 100-percent sure decision. If it appears that way, the family is probably not asking enough questions. Once family members have placed the decision in God's hands, they can make themselves available to carry it out with the information they have gathered from the above tools. The family should also have God's confirmation in their hearts for whatever choice they make.

## MEDICALLY NECESSARY ABORTION

In the United States, few issues since slavery and the Civil War have caused as much division as abortion has today—and with good reason. Any society that sees fit to steal the innocent lives of its young is destroying its future. The slippery slope of life-cheapening ethics will continue to drag that society to depths where life becomes meaningless and human carnage and slavery become common.

Scripture points toward Satan as the chief engineer of child slaughter through the ages. In Genesis, the serpent was cursed and told that it and man's "seed" would be at emnity for all time. "It will bruise thy head, and thou shalt bruise his heel" (Gen. 3:15). Satan must always strike at our seed, our most vulnerable and most defenseless part. In Egypt, and later in Israel, plots to destroy the children in order to prevent the birth of Moses (Ex. 1, 2) and of Jesus (Matt. 2:16–23) were also constructed. These plots developed in the hearts of despots who sought their own glory and the destruction of God's seed.

Under the Judeo-Christian ethic, many have understood and cherished children, raised them under the influence of Scripture and instilled in them values based on God's principles. The societal rebellion of the sixties led to the U.S. Supreme Court travesty of the seventies—the pronouncement that the interned child was merely a piece of tissue, disposable at any stage of development. They scoffed at the proofs of science that showed the child as a unique product of conception, human from its very beginning—breathing, feeding, needing care and nurture. Since then, the hardness of our social hearts and the ineffective voice of the church has led to continuing death of precious children.

It is currently becoming less popular to have a "convenience abortion."[6] Many women still desire the termination of a pregnancy for selfish reasons, however, and the term "medically necessary abortion" is becoming greatly overused. Proponents of abortion suggest that 10 percent of all abortions are medically necessary to save the life of the mother. The best figures that can be verified through National Right to Life and through

Critical Concern, a prolife physicians' group, suggest that far less than 1 percent are done for "true" medical necessity.

Much depends on how one manipulates the term "medically necessary." The abortion statistics from 1985 to 1988 suggest an average of 1.8 million abortions are accomplished every year.[7] The average number of live births per year is 3.3 million. The average number of deaths by all other causes is 1.9 million per year.[8] Approximately one-third of all pregnancies are ending in abortion, far above even the 10 percent claimed to be medically necessary.

Abortions that are necessary to save the mother at the child's expense are, fortunately, very rare. The most common form is a pregnancy in which the fertilized egg lodges and grows in a fallopian tube. One in a million of these children could survive until birth, and 99 percent of these pregnancies would probably kill the mother. The babies are often dead when the tubal pregnancy is removed. A medically necessary situation, this is often not considered abortion because the baby has already died.

Rarely, very rarely, a mother will have a life-threatening complication from diabetes, high-blood pressure, toxemia late in pregnancy, or a cancer. Many of these diseases are treatable today; and the woman, if she desires, can carry her child to term with proper medical care. The treatment for toxemia, for example, is to end the pregnancy. Toxemia does not usually occur until late in the pregnancy, however, and it is easy to save many of these children with our neonatal intensive care units. Conversely, the lifesaving treatment for uterine cancer in a pregnant woman may kill the child.

Abortions are also performed on children with severe, grotesque, life-threatening defects. Since almost all of these children will die before birth or shortly after, abortion is used to remove the child and the emotional sting of this tragedy. Since the child has already lost its ability to survive, this situation should not be used as an excuse to inflate the numbers of "medically necessary abortions."

When severe medical complications from a tubal pregnancy or cancer threaten both child and mother, the correct decision should be to prolong the life of the mother since both are likely to die if the problem continues. The woman should be counseled to grieve, but not to feel guilty or to blame herself for the baby's death. Before she goes through with any "medically necessary" abortion procedure, however, a prolife obstetrician or family physician should be consulted to show all possible medical options for saving her life *and* the child's. If no such options exist and the mother's life is at stake, we must educate her and help her to accept this situation so that she will look forward to bearing other children in the future. For additional help, see *Counseling for Unplanned Pregnancy and Infertility.*[9]

Please beware that many obstetricians would rather abort the baby than deal with a difficult, complicated pregnancy with high physical or legal risks. When they do suggest a "medically necessary" abortion, the counselor or pastor needs to counsel firmly, and lovingly, to seek a second, prolife opinion.

## LIFE-PROLONGING PROCEDURES

How do we decide on life-prolonging procedures? When are they correct? When are they harmful or destructive? Should we always trust the physician's opinion? What help can families obtain in making these decisions for a loved one?

No more difficult, emotionally charged, or devastating situation confronts an individual than having to decide the fate of another. Yet, if the ill patient and the decision-maker are both believers, the decision is only on the fate of the body, not the soul. Nonetheless, emotions are still likely to run high, even for Christians who know that the spiritual outcome is sure.

As suggested by the "Assessing Health Decisions" worksheet (see page 163), our primary concern is for the patient's spiritual condition. Prolonging the person's life may be more spiritually ethical if he or she has not made a decision for Christ. The family does not need to alert the physician to this "spiritual" reason for prolongation—he or she may then attempt to fight the family. The reasons the family members can give are simply that they want everything possible done or that they believe that the patient wanted every chance at life.

The spiritual condition should be pivotal when deciding whether to remove life-supporting equipment or pursue rigorous therapy, and all other medical, emotional, and personal complications should be secondary.

The patient's comfort should be of concern whether the family has decided to prolong the patient's life or not. Offering pain medication, providing respiratory support, and treating the medical problem will help. Comfort may be added to an unpleasant hospital bed by pillows, bed elevation, and padding for the elbows, heels, and back. Keeping the patient clean, shaved, and covered is important too. We must treat and communicate with dying people as if they are alert, can understand everything told them, and will recover completely.

Since many Christian families suffer through the agonizing decision to "terminate" their loved one by removing life-sustaining equipment, some facts need to be understood.

Life-sustaining equipment can keep the person alive only if his or her heart, lungs, and circulatory system are healthy, including the central area of the brain called the brainstem. The patient with a failing heart, lungs, or no brainstem function will soon die in spite of machines.

Only a very small percentage of patients declared brain-dead by electrical studies of the brain come back to a full mental existence. Yet some do. Prolonging these patients, however, will result in some who will remain in a totally non-functioning, "vegetable-like" state. Many patients would rather have their life support turned off than remain in such a condition. Hopefully, this desire will be known to the family before the prolongation results in this chronic vegetative state.

God is powerful enough to "call home" our loved ones if that is his desire. Since he can allow them to die even while on life support, we should never consider ourselves totally responsible for a family member's life. God is still in charge. We must look to him for guidance and comfort, while praying that he will soon end the situation through death or rapid recovery.

Those persons who desire to receive all life-sustaining treatments—medical, supportive, food, and hydration—might find it prudent to establish that fact with their physician and family by signing a "Life-Sustaining Procedures Declaration." A sample of this declaration, which is a legal document, is shown in Figure 8.

From a practical standpoint, what should our counsel be when we do not know the patient's spiritual status and when prolonging life is extremely uncomfortable for the patient? Taking a

I, ___(name)___, being at least eighteen (18) years old and of sound mind, willfully and voluntarily make known my desire that if at any time I have an incurable injury, disease, or illness determined to be a terminal condition I request the use of all medical procedure, treatments, and interventions that would extend my life (or delay my death) without regard to my physical or mental diagnosis, condition, or prognosis, and without regard to financial cost. This includes appropriate nutrition and hydration, the administration of medication, and the performance of all other medical procedures necessary to extend my life, to provide comfort and care, or to alleviate pain.

In the absence of my ability to give direction regarding the use of life-sustaining procedures, it is my intention that this declaration be honored by my family and physician as the expression of my legal right to request medical or surgical treatment and accept the consequences of the request. I understand the full import of this declaration.

Signed _____ Date _____

Address _____

The declarant has been personally known to me, and I believe (him/her) to be of sound mind. I am competent and at least eighteen (18) years old.

Witness _____ Date _____

Witness _____ Date _____

**Figure 8**
**Life-Sustaining Procedures Declaration[10]**

spiritual perspective, eternal pain and suffering are still worse than the present short-term suffering. In many situations, however, we do not know whether the patient will recover or if he or she has accepted Christ as Savior. Our counsel, therefore, should be to give the person every chance at recovery until the situation becomes hopeless or suffering increases and persists at high levels. If in doubt, suggest to the family to do what they would want done for them.

Situations may exist where IV fluids or feeding tubes should be withdrawn to hasten the death of a patient—leading to starvation and dehydration—but I have never seen such an instance as a physician, nor do I expect to see one. Removing life-supports, stopping certain medications, or abstaining from accomplishing a painful procedure can all be justified. But removing food and water from a patient has no biblical, ethical, or moral support unless the patient has explicitly left instructions for this to happen in certain medical conditions.

As Christians, it should be our responsibility to assist the patient by providing these basic needs until death. God will relieve the suffering in his perfect timing.

## EUTHANASIA

Some very sad cases have been reported in the past five years. One such case involved a woman dying of cancer who was supposedly in excruciating pain. Her husband could not bear to see her suffer any longer, so he pulled out a revolver and shot her in the head. He admitted to this act but stated that "Years in jail are well worth relieving her of her pain."

Other cases include situations where an overdosage of medication was given by a loving wife, by a "mercy-killing" nurse who was trying to free her patients from pain, and by a mother who helped her teenaged paraplegic son to kill himself. Were all of these the compassionate cases they were made out to be? Were any deaths excuses for abuse, hate, and revenge for the emotional pain caused to the killer?

Fortunately, the courts have consistently convicted mercy killers as the criminals they are. But how long will it be until we follow some of our European neighbors who already have laws to allow both passive and active euthanasia? Will we ever be killing defective newborns after birth just as we do before birth by abortion? Some countries have laws that newborns are not "children" for three days following birth. If the child dies by neglect or by medication in these first three days, then the death is viewed no differently than an abortion.

Scripture is just as clear by what it doesn't condone as by what it does. Jesus Christ, our Great Physician, never practiced, condoned, or participated in the premature death of another human being. Our ministry, like his, should be to ensure spiritual redemption, emotional well-being, and to the best of our ability, healing and caring for those who are physically ill.

Yet some very tempting questions remain. Why not allow a Christian who is suffering to die by neglect or with a hastening medication? Won't he be in heaven more quickly? Why doesn't the Bible mention euthanasia and suicide in the same terms as other unpardonable sins? Are they sins at all?

Another question may tempt the mind. Fighting for one's country is a noble cause, even though we are killing other people. Isn't helping a saint to reach heaven sooner, by relieving suffering, an even more noble cause?

Spring and Larson offer some answers:

> If God is sovereign and has given us the gift of life, then two truths are apparent: first, life is not ours to bestow or take. We cannot, in other words, "play God." Second, our stewardship over life must be consistent with God's intentions and purposes for our life. It is God's intention that we minister to others, share the Gospel with as many as we can, and witness of Christ's sufficiency through suffering or sickness. Suicide and euthanasia circumvent these scriptural calls to duty. The application, in the case of euthanasia, appears deceptively simple: we must never intervene to hasten our own or another's dying.[11]

Likewise, Solomon suggests that God appoints a time for man to die (Eccl. 3:2).

Temptations to compromise Scripture and to compromise these godly principles will always be present. The subtle suggestions to disobey these principles are as sinful as their end result. As a counselor, it is always wise to confirm these as worthwhile questions when counseling the family and openly discussing the arguments for and against withdrawing care. The counselor can then encourage the family to seek direct wisdom from God in prayer and the principles of Scripture.

## SUICIDE

We must immediately realize that the most common reason for a person to commit suicide is because of a treatable mental illness—depression. Depression, as discussed earlier, is often the result of biochemical changes in the emotional and central

171

areas of the brain.[12] Many types of stresses seem to precipitate these changes—physical illness, emotional stress, family dysfunction among them. But the bottom line is that suicide is preventable by early recognition of depression.

Other reasons may also explain why some are bent on self-destruction. Those entwined in satanic worship sacrifice animals, children, body parts, and even themselves. Other cults, such as the one at Jonestown, have elevated suicide as an essential means for protecting their religion. The Japanese culture, from the Buddhist tradition, has placed suicide in the defense of others as highly honorable. Some rock music promotes the worthlessness of life and the beauty of a suicidal death.

No matter the source, suicide always fulfills an evil desire for self-destruction. It is not condoned in Scripture as a way to relieve even intense suffering.

Any counselor who deals with suicidal patients quickly sees continued self-destructive behavior throughout the patient's lifetime. Many abuses—abuse of alcohol, abuse of illegal drugs, abuse of the body through sexual promiscuity or eating disorders, abuse of family—and a refusal to seek appropriate help or take medications properly are commonly seen behaviors in these self-destructive, self-hating individuals.[13] Counselors are often faced with complex situations where personality, relationships, and other emotional factors complicate overt depression.

Even Christians can commit suicide.

Upon returning from Christmas break, a student at a Christian college found his roommate suspended from a noose, hanging dead from the ceiling. The suicide note blamed his parents' divorce and his recent breakup with his girlfriend as the reasons for this self-destructive act. After reviewing his behavior over the break and previous semester, those nearest to him realized that the signs of depression were obvious.

A well-known Christian political figure was suffering from heart disease and from severe, painful rheumatoid arthritis, and attempting to live with little or no medication. One afternoon, his wife came home to find him slumped over a chair, a hole in his chest from their handgun.

In each of these suicides, depression was the result of emotional and physical stresses. Neither of these men had sought treatment for his suicidal thoughts. Neither had the capability of seeing past his own sorrow and troubles to find the help he needed. Yet each was responsible in the midst of troubles to seek an answer or help from his Savior.

I have had a number of Christian patients comment that the Lord directed them to my office for help with their suicidal and self-destructive thoughts. I tell them that scripturally, it is not the right choice to attempt to end a problem with suicide. Most problems can be corrected with further thought and prayer, but not after suicide. Many depressed people seem compelled to attempt suicide even though they know it is wrong. They do not have the strength to resist.

Counseling the family which has just lost a member to suicide may be the most difficult task you will be called upon to perform. Families may blame themselves for the stresses, poor relationships, or lack of recognition of the depression. We can help them diffuse their guilt by educating them about the biochemical causes of these abnormal thoughts. Lack of control over these thoughts is common, as is refusal to seek medical care. Few other diseases have symptoms that lead directly to a worsening of the illness, but depression causes retreat away from the people who can help.

We can also encourage the family from Scripture. Spiritually, there is no evidence that self-murder is a sin eternally separating us from God. For the Christian family and victim, we can be assured that their eternal spiritual fate is still secure, and they can still be found in the presence of the Lord.

Our greatest ministry to these depressed individuals and to their families is to prevent suicide through early detection, symptom recognition, and education of family members. Churches and youth groups offer an excellent place for teaching these preventative concepts and ministering to those in need.

# CHAPTER TEN

# SPIRITUAL FRUIT FROM ILLNESS

It is a typical Sunday morning in church. One family enters without the mother, who is to have her gall bladder removed the next morning. An elderly widow sits quietly across from this family, barely able to sit still because of joint pain. The young man in back has been undergoing chemotherapy for his leukemia, and is fortunate to have had so few side effects from the treatments. Another young woman has been unable to conceive because of previous infections and scarring. She and her husband remain angry, bitter, and unable to let the Word penetrate their suffering.

The family is very worried. The widow is in pain. The young man prays for a continued remission. The young woman prays for God's favor. Each is hearing Scripture take on new meaning. Each has been given a deeper understanding of suffering in life. Each could be found in your church or mine.

God is too loving *not* to allow us to suffer.

As we think of those people—the family, the elderly woman, the young man, and the young woman—it becomes our ministry to help them deal with their diseases, teaching and discipling them to accept and to grow. Yet our time and talents are limited. We, as counselors, pastors, and physicians, cannot meet all of the needs created or driven by their illness. Instead, many Christian professionals have "burned out," expecting to meet all of the needs given to them.

We will offer a greater ministry to our patients if we learn to use our talents in the counseling realm and delegate other areas of ministry to those gifted by God to accomplish them. Many churches have dear ladies who minister without fanfare in the homes of the ill.

As Marty and Vaux point out, "The congregation has certain unique resources to bring to people in illness and health and all who care about them in varied ways."[1]

We are also to call the "elders," representatives of the congregation, to anoint the one who is sick and pray with faith on behalf of the congregation[2] (James 5:14). Our churches and our people will be better served if we all enter into the biblical admonition of ministering to our sick and infirm.

Let us examine some practical aspects of ministering to those who are ill. If there are no such ministries in your church, perhaps you could be instrumental in starting them.

### CHURCH-BASED MINISTRIES

The Christian patient from a loving church rooted in ministries of mercy is often smothered with visits, cards, letters, flowers, balloons, and food, as well as meals and care for the rest of the family. This can be one of the most spiritually maturing times for believers who are emotionally rocked by illness or filled with spiritual doubt. But they may be so overwhelmed by the support from their church that accepting the illness as God's purpose becomes painless. They grow so much from this encouragement that their illness is less prolonged. It is great to be a part of a church like this, a truly caring Christian community.

The church often benefits as well. It puts aside squabbles and fights to stay up all night praying for an infirm brother or sister. The people share a common broken heart as they grieve and suffer with the sick patient. In our own ministry, I have seen the church become as one: Everyone in the congregation has prayed for the sick person and helped the family to cope. The church can become a truly extended family. We feel responsible for our loved ones and will go out of our way to help.

The church that does not demonstrate this outpouring of love for its ill members misses much. The hearts of its people will grow cold, caring only for their own individual needs. The outreach ministry to others will often dry up instead of being blessed to "overflowing" (Mal. 3:10). Our society suffers today because of such cold-hearted churches.

Getting people involved in the pain and suffering of others, allowing them the privilege of crying with the broken and infirm, and sharing the burdens of meeting simple, basic family needs will do much for a church. Involvement will melt their "heart of stone" and allow the Lord to replace it with a caring, soft, pliable "heart of flesh" (Ezek. 11:19). The pastor and support staff, the professional counselor, and other health professionals within the church can help congregation members see what they are missing.

Here are some practical suggestions for laying the groundwork for a health ministry in your church starting with the most commonly found ministry, a visitation ministry.

### Visitation Ministry

Scripture calls us to help those who cannot help themselves—the sick, the widows, the orphans, and those in jail (Matt. 25:34–40; James 1:27). It has long been a tradition for the pastor to visit the sick and infirmed, and to bring comfort through holding a hand, reading Scripture, encouragement, and prayer. Much comfort can be derived from the caring relationship a pastor offers.

In our fast-paced society, however, the visit may take on only token, superficial proportions. With so many responsibilities, it is difficult for a pastor to spend more than a few minutes with a hospital patient or a shut-in. The conversation becomes rigid and rehearsed because both patient and pastor need to "move on." Does this type of visitation express the love and care desired by the patient? Both patient and pastor may be more anxious because of the brevity of the visit than relieved by the kindness intended.

A hallmark of a true, caring visitation ministry is being able to spend unlimited time to meet the needs of the patient. Those who minister offer an unhurried, loving, empathetic demeanor.

A simple question to ask yourself is, "Am I offering enough time to counsel this patient's needs?" If you are not, you do not have enough time to visit, either. Sufficient time for a visit is the same as for a counseling session. Although the visit may be shortened by the patient's desire for solitude, be prepared and willing to offer as much time as he or she needs.

Be ever mindful of the condition of the patient—physically, emotionally, and spiritually. The patient may be so exhausted from testing that a visit will be too difficult. Always ask, as you enter, if the time is appropriate and comfortable for a visit. Sensitivity to a distraught or tiring patient is essential, and returning at a better time will be much appreciated. Remember that illness is the most opportune time to offer spiritual solutions for a patient's problems, but we must be caring enough not to force spiritual food into a closed mouth.

A full visitation ministry requires more than just pastoral visits to the ill. It requires participation by the entire church (Matt. 25:34–40), which may take many steps to initiate or improve health ministry, perhaps as part of a broader visitation ministry:[3]

1. Take another church member with you to give that person training and experience when you visit the sick or make hospital rounds.
2. Assign hospital visits to the deacon staff, two at a time.
3. Have a group within the church organize visits, flowers, cards, and meals for the family, and—in a prolonged illness—help with cleaning and child care.

4. In all Sunday school classes, assign one person to visit sick class members and organize help to meet some of these other physical needs.

5. Have classes to train volunteers to "adopt" a chronically ill person, helping him or her deal with emotional needs, assisting with physical problems, and being a spiritual encourager.

6. Have a special prayer sheet for the ill that can be handed out at worship services to allow the whole congregation to pray and show concern for the patient and family.

7. Speak of health concerns from the pulpit, making sure to give only the information that the patient or family has authorized you to pronounce.

8. Organize a benevolence fund to help with the cost of medication or treatment. It is essential that the patient be able to take medication or treatments to recover and eventually, perhaps, pay back the others in a similar manner.

9. Organize prayer chains specifically for immediate health needs.

10. Have the pastor, secretary, Sunday school teacher, or some other designated person continue to contact the patient for updates and prayer requests until the treatments are through and a full recovery obtained.

These are simple suggestions that many churches already use to meet needs through visitation and mercy ministry. As you can see, they cost little to the church except voluntary time, loving effort, and sacrificial giving.

## Counseling Ministry

It is the purpose of this text and others in the Resources for Christian Counseling series to extend the ministry of the pastor to include the psychological needs of church members. Historically, churches have offered food, shelter, clothing, and comfort to their flocks as well as ministry to those in need. The spiritual needs have always received top-priority—teaching, preaching, and counseling have given spiritual insight and wisdom. However, it has not been until this century that the church has organized any ministry to meet the specific psychological needs of its members. The need for a Christian perspective on psychology has grown tremendously as the psychiatric and scientific psychological communities have based their therapies and philosophies in "anti-Christian" humanism. The offering of psychological counsel has become an important ministry for many pastors.[4]

Although the scope of this book is far too limited to deal fully with all types of counseling ministries, a few comments are warranted.

The practice of the counselor can take on many sizes and shapes. Pastors trained to give spiritual and psychological counsel often use their own offices to counsel on a part-time basis. Some churches are hiring full-time counselors to join other staff members in handling the psychological needs of the church. Some pastors spend a few hours a day counseling in a physician's office, a professional setting where fees are routinely charged. Other Christian counselors may join together to form a counseling group. They rent space, charge for services, and maintain educational and media ties to enhance their practice. Many in these counseling groups maintain pastoral duties at local churches while working part-time for the counseling group.

Though professional training and charging for services have enhanced the image of Christian counseling, the ministry of counseling should not be despised or put aside. Sitting with a dying patient all night because the family is just too tired, getting calls at all hours of the day or night to soothe crisis situations, offering to see non-paying patients, helping a family understand the seriousness of a medical problem—all demonstrate the caring of the counseling ministry. The world will be impressed by our degree, our knowledge, and our practice; our patients will be impressed by our caring, our advice, and our sacrifice to meet their needs.

## Medical Ministry

A review of medical history shows the church of the Middle Ages was the keeper of potions, concoctions, and remedies.[5] The pastor was viewed as the civilized "medicine-man" for his tribe. Churches in this century, however, have exchanged the ministry of providing medical care to almost shunning the medical needs of people. Many congregations actively give food, clothing, and shelter, but rare is the church that gives medical care to the indigent, displaced people who seek its help. Many church-sponsored hospitals have closed their doors, been swallowed up by other corporations, or put aside their spiritual emphasis in exchange for a purely scientific one.

The resurgence of volunteerism within American culture in this past decade has opened doors for churches to broaden their mercy ministries into the health area and may offer a model that can be applied elsewhere. Physicians, nurses, pharmacists, dentists, and other health professionals are donating time to various church-sponsored programs that offer free care to the indigent. The usual model for this is a church-based "free clinic." The church is responsible for the organization, the space, the donated time, the donated medications and supplies, and the distribution of times or appointments to those in need. This is a large endeavor and requires a large volunteer pool or a smaller, but more dedicated, group.

There are several ways for a pastor to solicit local physicians to become involved with a medical ministry.[6]

1. Ask local physicians if you can refer a non-paying medical need to their office as you are made aware of the need. The pastor should assure the physician that only patients introduced by the pastor and confirmed as real needs will be referred. This offers the physician protection from opening "the indigent door." News travels quickly about a doctor who will see anyone without charge.

2. A physician may seek to have his practice come under the authority of the local church. The practice will be dedicated, the church will pray for it, and it will serve the needs of the local congregation. A portion of the money earned will be given as a tithe to the church.[7]

3. Christian physicians may seek referral of Christian patients to their practice with the help of local pastors.

4. A large church or ministry can open its own clinic within the church complex. It can hire the physicians, nurses, and

office staff, and buy or lease the necessary equipment to run it as a non-profit business that benefits the church. Church members, neighbors, and those too poor to pay can all be seen, and funds can be generated to offset costs.[8]

5. After opening a clinic, several physicians can be hired. This increases the funds collected, and some may be put aside for medical missions. One nurse and physician from the group can be constantly on the mission field, while others minister in the local church-based clinic.[9]

## MINISTRY-BASED PROGRAMS

So many churches and ministries have counseling or health-related programs that it will be impossible to describe, or even list, all of the good ones and their innovations. Ministry-based programs can be initiated by a local church, and sustained through separate fund raising, with money allocated for specific functions of that ministry. Christian psychiatric hospitals and medical clinics, for example, may originate in a local church, but then become separate, raising their own funds and acting autonomously.

One example of this genre of ministry is that of ELIM Home for Alcoholic Men, which provides a six-week, intensive, spiritual behavioral modification program. It is funded totally by Thomas Road Baptist Church and remains a part of that broad ministry. Many sub-ministries like ELIM Home take enormous resources and are practical only when part of larger ministries or when they grow into separate, self-sufficient entities.

### Practical Needs Ministry

Many evangelical churches are helping to meet the day-to-day needs of the indigent, poor, or unfortunate within their communities. It is not a new idea. In fact, it may be the oldest mission of the New Testament church (Acts 2:45, 46; 6:1–7). In recent days, however, it has arrived in different, unusual packaging.

A commonly used concept is that of the "family store."[10] Food, clothing, medication, appliances, toiletries, and other basic necessities are donated from local businesses and individuals. A family with certain needs is invited to "shop" the store to find what it needs. Both over-the-counter medication and prescriptions can be offered if a pharmacist is available for dispensing and if the medication has been donated. There is little or no charge for meeting these needs. The aspect of coming into a store and shopping for these necessities lends some dignity to an otherwise demeaning situation.

Often churches that run these stores have a trained pastoral or counseling staff available to discuss the family's spiritual and psychological needs as well as its material needs for survival. This provides an excellent opportunity for a church to offer the spiritual and emotional help that is so commonly needed after catastrophic losses—such as loss of a job, or loss of housing.

Many churches have a benevolence offering to help meet the needs of the unfortunate in their congregation or their community. These monies can be used to buy food and clothing, to meet medical needs, or to pay for psychological or crisis counseling if they are unavailable through the church.

## Companionship Ministry

Scripturally, we are called to honor and care for our parents. Yet often elderly or handicapped individuals are left to take care of themselves. They may not have sufficient funds to move into a group home, or they may desire not to leave their home. Often their isolation and loneliness leads to depression and poor self care.

Just as the early church was charged to minister to the widows, so today's churches should be willing and organized to care for their own infirm or aged. Some churches have separate offices to coordinate transportation, meals, physician visits, counseling visits, and other needs for their elderly and handicapped.[11] Others rely on the unorganized (but often efficient) voluntary mercy-showers—the people who always seem to know who has needs, to recognize what they are, and to have the time to meet them.

Supplying the companionship needs of the handicapped and elderly through visitations or counseling can keep many of them from becoming depressed or feeling left out. Group activities for senior adults are beneficial in keeping them active and energetic. Single adults who can live temporarily with an elderly or infirm person while their family is on vacation can relieve much of the worry the family has about leaving. Visiting nursing-home patients falls within this area of ministry as well.

## Abuse Ministries

Unfortunate as it is, child abuse and wife abuse are common, dangerous situations that occur within our society and our churches. If the child or wife is not removed, serious physical trauma or death can result. Though rare in many smaller towns, many large cities have often set up shelters to house and protect these battered people.[12]

A church can let the local police department know that it is willing to help with this problem by providing shelter or funds. Keeping a list of homes or people who are willing to become involved on a moment's notice may be all the organization that is needed. Be sure that the host family has adequate protection.

## Telephone Counseling

Many organizations and churches are setting up toll-free lines to help meet the needs of their town or city. These can range from minimally trained "referral" counselors who will call the appropriate people, to highly trained crisis counselors who will staff the phones full time. They can answer everything from spiritual questions about salvation to where people may go for their next meal. The telephone number must be well publicized in the phone book, advertisements, stores, public areas, and other churches.[13]

## Medical Referral

In an unfortunate situation, a member of your church may need medical care but be unable to pay. Keeping a list of local physicians who would be willing to help in these crisis times will give you the ability to call them when need arises. Many physicians would be glad to help, especially if the call comes from a pastor and especially if the church promises to pay for any medication or therapies needed to cure the problem.

Christian physicians may be interested in looking for Christian patients, or vice versa. Helping these two to meet represents a ministry to both.

This ministry can also be expanded to include a broad range of health categories—specialists, special therapies, general information, self-help groups, and local hospital information. Collecting the information is an ongoing, ever-changing process, but it is not that difficult for a secretary to do. Making sure that your people, other churches, and the rest of the community know the referral phone number will minister to your city or town.

### Abortion/Adoption Referral

Training your "toll-free" or medical referral counselors to discuss the options of adoption rather than convenience abortion can also provide a great service to distraught young women seeking answers. Many are given misleading information by abortion counselors who tell them it is the "simplest" solution. But they may want to discuss other alternatives when they do not feel comfortable with the abortion option.

Providing counselors a separate hot line, or a pastor or professional counselor to return the young woman's call can give her all the necessary information. Ministries can expand these services into testing for pregnancy and providing medical care, clothing, food, and shelter. Some may be able to offer full "maternity home" programs that care for the young mother until delivery. Having an adoption service nearby also fulfills an important need because approximately 50 percent of these young mothers will opt to put their babies up for adoption after delivery.[14]

### AIDS Ministry

One of the future areas of ministry will be to meet the medical and psychological needs of those who have AIDS. Present statistics suggest that between 1.5 and 3 million people are already infected with the AIDS virus and will probably die from the disease within five to ten years. Most of those infected come from three groups—homosexual men, intravenous drug users, and hemophiliacs. But a recent study from the U.S. Centers for Disease Control in Atlanta, Georgia, and the American College Health Association proves that AIDS is spreading rapidly among heterosexual college students. This disease may

present one of the greatest ministry challenges of our generation—helping these people with their physical, psychological,
and spiritual needs.

What types of ministry can be offered for those with AIDS?
As mentioned before, we can help to meet such physical needs
as food, clothing, necessities, and medication against the disease or its consequences. Almost all of the victims have guilt
about their sexual habits or drug abuse that causes grief and
anger, and needs psychological and spiritual counsel.

Many homosexuals or intravenous drug users will be wary
or unwilling to listen to a professional counselor or pastor.
Their minds and hearts have been so seared that they will only
trust those who are addicted as they are (Rom. 1:26, 27).
Co-counseling the AIDS victim has proven successful when a
pastor or counselor, along with a converted homosexual or IV-
drug user, together attempt to break this defensive shell built
to protect the sinner and his sin.[15]

The ultimate counsel needed is spiritual counsel. During
these severe trials, even the most rebellious may seek God's
deliverance. He or she may be open to the gospel of Christ and
the forgiveness it offers. The loving and caring demeanor of the
counselor will be the quickest way to change hatred toward
the Gospel into a more open consideration of the claims of
Christ.

How do we counsel those who have innocently contracted the
AIDS infection through blood transfusion, through an unfaith-
ful or bisexual spouse, or through ministering in a foreign country? To innocently contract a "disease of sin" may seem like the
most unfair situation imaginable. Yet our answers must speak of
the scriptural principles showing a loving, forgiving God who
must judge the sin of this world. Since we all are sinners and
deserve death, it is by God's grace that we are allowed to live at
all. The issue of fairness will be clarified from the Judge's
mouth while we spend eternity with him.

The major difficulty in setting up an AIDS ministry is to
define the level of care to offer. It is safe to visit with, pray with,
clean the apartment of, or run errands for an AIDS patient. A
few simple precautions are recommended for those ministering
to AIDS patients:

1. Do not visit an AIDS patient if you are sick or have a respiratory illness. You are far more dangerous to someone with little or no immune function than he or she is to you. Your simple diseases could kill the AIDS patient.
2. Cover all your sores or cuts with an antibiotic ointment and a bandage before cleaning or helping around the patient's house or apartment.
3. Do not clean any secretions or blood, or take care of any medical appliances, if you are not properly trained in infectious disease protection.
4. Remember AIDS is not spread by casual contact, but it has been spread through blood, secretions, breast milk, sharing of intravenous needles, and sexual contact.

Probably churches can best become involved with the AIDS problem through education. Approximately 80 percent of parents do not teach their children about sexuality or addictive drugs. Teens and children are learning from the drug pushers or those who want to have sex. A recent bumper sticker suggests the solution: "It's about time that PARENTS become the pushers." We must encourage our parents to become involved with education before AIDS spreads more widely through our teen heterosexual population.

Churches can sponsor educators and speakers on the topics of AIDS and sexuality, to speak with and train parents and equip them to train their children.[16] Public education about sex and AIDS almost never mentions the term "abstinence," unless it is used as a last resort—an almost laughable afterthought. Churches should not be saddled with the sole responsibility for teaching biblical sexuality. Instead, schools and churches should encourage parents to become active in teaching their children at home, where role models and values are taught and seen.

## SPIRITUAL WITNESS TO HEALTH CARE PROFESSIONALS

During their professional lifetimes, physicians and nurses will take care of hundreds of dying patients who could choose Christ on their deathbeds. Spending time evangelizing medical professionals within your community may have exciting eternal consequences because of their strategic, trusted position in people's lives.

Health care professionals, however, may also be the toughest group to reach. Their training is filled with the secular philosophies of humanism, ethical relativism, and belief in the "all-powerful god of science." They are highly intelligent, self-reliant, and strongly motivated to believe in themselves and their skills. They are also very busy people who have great demands put on their working and free time.

Evangelizing physicians requires a strategy. Seeing your private physician for a visit gives you an open door to offer him or her a special gift for being so kind and helpful. Let me suggest giving them the Campus Crusade tract "Jesus and the Intellectuals," by itself or preferably with another gift (food gifts are usually appreciated). I have found this tract to be one of the best for medical professionals. Taking this same opportunity to share Christ with nurses and other staff is also helpful. Leaving your business card or church card will give them a reminder to possibly attend your church.

As with other busy business people, you may need to make a special appointment over lunch or in their office. Using this opportunity to ask for help with a health ministry or free clinic is a good way to get your foot in the door—and for the physician to see how you care for and minister to others. This witness of this active ministry can lead to other opportunities to share the plan of salvation directly with the physician.

Asking hospitalized patients to give their doctors tracts or gifts during their morning rounds is another way of sharing the Gospel. Packaging the tract so that it can be slipped into a shirt pocket will offer the best chance of having it looked at.

A church can set up a conference for local physicians, asking a Christian physician to speak on a topic of medical interest as well as share his or her faith. Physicians will often attend a talk or lecture if continuing medical education (CME) credit is given or if refreshments are available. The church can also make a low-pitch plea for help with a specific ministry.

One very successful way to reach the intellectual person is through dinner meetings with well-known Christian personalities addressing the group. Funds for such endeavors can come through other Christian business people and professionals in your community.[17]

Many other ways can be devised to evangelize health care professionals in your area as suggested in the following list.

1. Send letters of invitation to services along with a tract to the entire medical community.
2. Call and arrange a "house-call" where the pastor comes to visit the physician and his or her family. Offers from the church to help needy patients should catch the ear of the physician.
3. Send the physicians in your community Christmas cards that stress your "pro-life" leanings and ministry. Make sure you include your phone number if you are willing to counsel patients for adoption instead of abortion.
4. Let a physician's office know that you can be called if a patient cannot afford an essential prescription so that the church and a local pharmacy can together meet the need. When he or she calls, use it as an opportunity to offer the gospel as well.

It would take another book to discuss all of the various health care ministries or ideas for such ministries. Not much has yet been published in this area except for anecdotal accounts in general religious magazines. The future holds many new, exciting approaches for our churches and their ministries.

---

# EMOTIONAL SUPPORT CARE PLAN

The counselor may reproduce this questionnaire, or any portion of it, for use in the counseling session.

Many health professionals use care plans to insure a standard of quality for hospital patients, nursing home patients, and outpatient care. This care plan offers a framework from which the counselor can design counseling sessions that best meet the ill patient's needs. It sets out the issues of illness in an orderly fashion. Using it to discuss patient expectations, fears, support systems, and recovery goals will soften the impact of hospitalization and illness.

## USE

The counselor may want to give the patient a copy of the "Emotional Reactions to Illness" questionnaire, circling the number of any questions he or she wishes the patient to think about. During future sessions, these questions can be discussed in depth. These discussions should reduce anxiety and fear associated with the hospitalization, the diagnosis, the losses pertaining to the illness, and the permanent changes in lifestyle and psychological state that the illness may bring.

## EMOTIONAL REACTIONS TO ILLNESS

A. *What are your expectations about the illness?*
   1. What details have you discussed with your physician about the reason you are being hospitalized?
   2. Have you been given any expectations about how long you will be hospitalized or what the results are likely to be?
   3. Has the physician discussed your tests or the reason they are necessary? Has he or she warned you of any discomfort?
   4. What does your family or support system know about the problem, the reason for hospitalization, or the tests?
   5. What are you expecting the test results will be?
   6. Have you prepared yourself for either a serious diagnosis or a benign diagnosis?
   7. Have you ever been hospitalized? If not, has the hospital or the nursing staff helped you become acclimated to the environment?
   8. Have you brought any personal articles to help make your stay more pleasant and give you more comfort?

B. *What are your fears about the illness?*
   1. What do you fear most about being in the hospital?
   2. Does your family know about your fears or understand them? Are they willing to help you reduce them?
   3. Have you discussed your fears with your physician?
   4. Are you fearing a serious diagnosis? If so, what specific things are you afraid to lose?
   5. Are you afraid about how you will react to a serious diagnosis?

6. Do you fear the pain associated with the testing or the illness? Have you discussed pain medication with your physician?

7. What does your family fear about this illness? Have you discussed their fears with them?

8. Are other family problems coming to mind (such as relationship problems, guilt, or anger) because of the illness? Are you afraid to deal with these problems?

9. Will you or your family have any problems if you have a benign diagnosis or nothing is found causing the problem?

C. *Who comprises your support system?*

1. How will your family handle their daily schedule while you are ill? Have you discussed necessary adjustments with them?

2. Do you have sufficient financial resources during this illness to make sure basic needs are met?

3. How would you like your family (including your extended family) to support you during your illness? In the hospital? At home?

4. Have you discussed how often visits will be made, and by whom? Are the children allowed to visit? When?

5. Will you need support from pastor or church during or after your hospitalization? Have you called your pastor and discussed your illness?

6. Would you mind if the church helps you or your family with meals, errands, cleaning, odd jobs, funds, or their prayers?

7. Would you prefer that certain people did not know about your illness? Who and why?

8. Have you notified your supervisor at work? Have arrangements been made to fulfill your responsibilities? Will there be lost income, disability papers to file, a potential loss of your job, demotion, or other changes at work due to this illness? How do you feel about these things?

9. Do you have any other financial, psychological, or

spiritual support systems that can help you or your family during this illness? Are there any government agencies, self-help groups, educational groups, or research groups that can give you information or financial support?

D. *What are your goals for recovery?*
   1. Have you discussed your recovery and rehabilitation with your physician or with your physical therapist?
   2. Do you have a plan for rehabilitation? Have you set short-term, obtainable goals? Do you have a means of charting your progress?
   3. Are there any factors you know of that might slow down your recovery—physical, emotional, or spiritual factors? Are there any relationship problems or financial problems?
   4. Are there things that might speed up your progress if they were available to you?
   5. What emotional reasons make you want to recover?
   6. What emotional factors make it better for you to stay disabled?
   7. Will you be on disability? How long? Are there any rules for its continuation?
   8. Do you expect a complete recovery, a return to normal function? Have you been warned that complete recovery is unlikely or impossible? Has the physician told you how much of a loss to expect?
   9. Will you be able to return to your present job? What will happen if you cannot?
   10. How would you feel about an incomplete recovery? Do you blame anyone for this problem? How will you resolve such issues of blame? Were there factors beyond your control or the control of the party to blame? Have you forgiven that person or situation? When will you forgive them? Is the lack of forgiveness hampering your recovery?
   11. Are you taking responsibility for the cause and recovery of the disease process? If not, why not? Who else should take responsibility for your recovery and treatments?

E. *What are your feelings about yourself and your illness?*

1. Can you express your feelings about the disease, the treatment, any perceived losses, and your recovery? How do you usually express your feelings? With whom do you discuss your feelings?

2. Have you resolved any spiritual issues because of this illness? Do you feel God is unfair to you or others? Why do you feel this way? Do you understand the infirmities of Pharaoh, Job, Isaiah, Paul, or Christ? Do you understand the need for suffering in the life of a believer?

3. How do others in your family deal with illness—your parents, your spouse, your extended family? How has your pastor or others in your church dealt with a serious illness?

4. How do you feel about the quality of your care from the hospital staff, your physician, specialists, or the business office? Will you continue to use these health care providers? If not, why not? Did you receive a second opinion before treatment or surgery?

5. Have you been treated unfairly or with a lack of sensitivity by anyone in the health care team? If so, by whom? Have you discussed your treatment with them and how they can better treat you or others in the future?

6. How will you feel if you are given six months to live? What preparations will you need to make to get a second opinion? Are there ways for you to feel better for a longer period of time?

7. How will you feel if you are told you must deal with this problem for the rest of your life? What plans will need to be made for continuing care? How will your lifestyle change? Will your family, support system, or job change?

8. Are you prepared for a chronic, slowly progressive illness with which you must deal every day? How will you prepare yourself emotionally for the pain, the necessary care, and the changes you would have to make?

# BIBLIOGRAPHY

The following compilation contains information on counseling the sick, grieving, and terminally ill. It represents a broad, diverse selection of the most recent literature available for those who desire more readings on this topic in texts with proven excellent information. Word Publishing does not endorse, nor necessarily agree with, all material contained herein. This list is provided for the reader who needs to understand many different points of view on this important topic.

## COUNSELING THE SICK PERSON

Becker, A. H. *The Compassionate Visitor: Resources for Ministering to People Who Are Ill.* Minneapolis, Minn.: Augsburg Publishing House, 1985.

Field, M. *Patients Are People: A Medical-Social Approach to Prolonged Illness.* New York: Columbia University Press, 1953.

Friedman, J. *Home Health Care: A Guide for the Patient and Their Family.* New York: Norton, 1986.

Green, S. A. *Mind and Body: The Psychology of Physical Illness.* Washington, D.C.: American Psychiatric Press, 1985.

Jaco, E. G. *Patients, Physicians and Illness.* New York: The Free Press, 1972.

Lambert and Lambert. *Psychosocial Care of the Physically Ill: What Every Nurse Should Know.* 2d ed. Englewood Cliffs, N.J.: Prentice-Hall, 1985.

Scherzer, C. J. *Ministering to the Physically Sick.* Englewood Cliffs, N.J.: Prentice-Hall, 1963.

Shaw, N. S. *Humanizing Health Care: Task of the Patient Representative.* Oradell, N.J.: Medical Economics, 1980.

Twaddle, A. C. *Sickness Behavior and the Sick Role.* Boston: G. K. Hall, 1979.

## STRESS, ILLNESS, AND THE IMMUNE SYSTEM

Calabrese, J. R. "Alterations in Immunocompetence During Stress, Bereavement, and Depression: Focus on Neuroendocrine Regulation." *American Journal of Psychiatry.* 144 (1987): 1123–34.

Cousins, N. *Anatomy of an Illness.* Toronto: Bantam Books, 1979.

Cronenberger, J. H. *Immunology: Basic Concepts, Diseases and Laboratory Methods.* East Norwalk, Conn.: Appleton and Lange, 1988.

Paul, W. E. *Fundamental Immunology.* New York: Raven Publications, 1986.

Plotnikoff, M. P. *Enkephalins and Endorphins: Stress and the Immune System.* New York: Plenum Publishers, 1986.

Roitt, I. M. *Essential Immunology.* 6th ed. Chicago: Year Book Medical, 1988.

## GRIEF AND DEATH COUNSELING

Bane, J. D. *Death and Ministry: Pastoral Care of the Dying and the Bereaved.* New York: The Seabury Press, 1975.

Bowers, M. K. *Counseling the Dying.* New York: Jason Aronson, 1976.

Bugen, L. A. *Death and Dying: Theory/Research/Practice.* Dubuque, Iowa: William C. Brown, 1979.

Estadt, B. K. *Pastoral Counseling.* Englewood Cliffs, N.J.: Prentice-Hall, 1983.

Hagglund, T. B. *Dying: A Psychoanalytic Study with Special Reference to Individual Creativity and Defense Organization.* New York: International Universities Press, 1978.

Kalish, R. *Death, Grief, and Caring Relationships.* 2d ed. Monterey, Calif.: Brooks/Cole, 1985.

Kalish, R. *The Final Transition.* Amityville, N.Y.: Baywood, 1987.

Koop, R. L. *Encounter with Terminal Illness.* Grand Rapids, Mich.: Zondervan, 1980.

Kübler-Ross, E. *On Death and Dying.* New York: Macmillan, 1969.

———. *Death: The Final Stage of Growth.* Englewood Cliffs, N.J.: Prentice-Hall, 1975.

Parkes, C. M. *Bereavement.* New York: International Universities Press, 1972.

———. *Recovery from Bereavement.* New York: Basic Books, 1983.

Rando, T. A. *Grief, Dying, and Death: Clinical Interventions for Caregivers.* Champaign, Ill.: Research Press, 1984.

Soulen, R. N. *Care for the Dying.* Atlanta: John Knox Press, 1975.

Standachen, C. *Beyond Grief: A Guide for Recovering from the Death of a Loved One.* Oakland, Calif.: New Harbinger, 1987.

Weizman and Kamm. *About Mourning: Support and Guidance for the Bereaved.* New York: Human Sciences Press, 1985.

Worden, J. W. *Grief Counseling and Grief Therapy.* New York: Springer, 1982.

## HOSPICE AND TERMINAL ILLNESS

Goldberg, I. K. *Pain, Anxiety and Grief: Pharmacotherapeutic Care of the Dying Patient and the Bereaved.* New York: Columbia University Press, 1985.

Mummley, A. *The Hospice Alternative: A New Context for Death and Dying.* New York: Basic Books, 1983.

O'Connor, B. *The Role of the Minister in the Caring for the Dying Patient and the Bereaved.* Salem, N.H.: Ayer, 1985.

## LEGAL AND ETHICAL ISSUES OF PROLONGATION

Douders, A. E. *Legal and Ethical Aspects of Treating Critically and Terminally Ill Patients.* Ann Arbor, Mich.: Health Administration Press, 1982.

Goulden, P. *Medical Science and the Law.* rev. ed. New York: Facts on File Publications, 1984.

Johnson, S. H. *Long Term Care and the Law.* Owings Mills, Md.: National Health Publishing, 1983.

Laben, J. K. *Legal Issues and Guidelines: For Nurses Who Care for the Mentally Ill.* Thorofare, N.J.: SLACK, 1984.

Meador, B. D. *The Critically Ill.* Oradell, N.J.: Medical Economics, 1985.

Scully, T. *Playing God: The New World of Medical Choices.* New York: Simon and Schuster, 1988.

Walton, D. N. *Ethics of Withdrawal of Life-Support Systems: Case Studies in Decision Making in Intensive Care.* New York: Praeger, 1987.

## SUICIDE

Klerman, G. L. *Suicide and Depression.* Washington, D.C.: American Psychiatric Press, 1986.

Linzer, N. *Suicide: The Will to Live vs. the Will to Die.* New York: Human Sciences Press, 1984.

Madison, A. *Suicide among Young People.* New York: Clarion Books, 1978.

Shniedman, E. *Definition of Suicide.* New York: John Wiley and Sons, 1985.

# NOTES

## Chapter 1  The Response to Illness

1. Stephen A. Green, *Mind and Body: The Psychology of Physical Illness* (Washington, D.C.: American Psychiatric Press, Inc., 1985). Andrew C. Twaddle, *Sickness Behavior and the Sick Role* (Boston: G. K. Hall and Company, 1979). E. G. Jaco, *Patients, Physicians and Illness* (New York: The Free Press, 1972). N. S. Shaw, *Humanizing Health Care: Task of the Patient Representative* (Oradell, N.J.: Medical Economics Company, 1980). Lambert and Lambert, *Psychosocial Care of the Physically Ill: What Every Nurse Should Know*, 2d ed. (Englewood Cliffs, N.J.: Prentice-Hall, 1985). Minna Field, *Patients Are People: A Medical-Social Approach to Prolonged Illness* (Morningside Heights, N.Y.: Columbia University Press, 1953).

2. Hackett and Cassem, *Handbook of General Hospital Psychiatry* (St. Louis: C. V. Mosby, 1978), 266–273. Lawrence C. Kolb, *Modern Clinical Psychiatry* (W. B. Saunders and Company, 1977), 550–551. Gary R. Collins, *Christian Counseling: A Comprehensive Guide* (Waco, Tex.: Word, 1980), 401–402.

3. Stephen A. Green, *Mind and Body: The Psychology of Physical Illness* (Washington, D.C.: American Psychiatric Press, 1985).

4. Felix Deutsch, "Euthanasia: A Clinical Study," *Psychoanalysis Quarterly* 5 (1936):347–368. K. R. Eissler, *The Psychiatrist*

198

*and the Dying Patient* (New York: International Universities Press, 1955). B. Sanford, "Some Notes on a Dying Patient," *Journal of Psychoanalysis* 33 (1952):142–155. F. Joseph, "Transference and Countertransference in the Case of a Dying Patient," *Psychoanalysis and Psychoanalytic Review* 49, no. 4 (1962):21–34. J. Norton, "Treatment of a Dying Patient" in *The Psychoanalytic Study of the Child* (New York: International Universities Press, 1963), 541–560.

5. Sigmund Freud, *Thoughts for the Times on War and Death: Part II, Our Attitudes toward Death,* Standard Edition (London: Hogarth Press, 1957), 289–300.

6. Tor-Bjorn Hagglund, *Dying: A Psychoanalytic Study with Special Reference to Individual Creativity and Defense Organization* (New York: International Universities Press, 1978), 17.

7. Elisabeth Kübler-Ross, *On Death and Dying* (New York: Macmillan, 1969).

8. J. R. Averill, "Grief: Its Nature and Significance," *Psychological Bulletin* 70 (1968):721–748.

9. Colin M. Parkes, *Bereavement* (New York: International Universities Press, 1972).

10. Richard A. Kalish, *Death, Grief, and Caring Relationships,* 2d ed. (Monterey, Calif.: Brooks/Cole Publishing Company, 1985), 184.

11. Weizman and Kamm, *About Mourning: Support and Guidance for the Bereaved* (New York: Human Sciences Press, 1985), 42–63.

12. William Worden, *Grief Counseling and Grief Therapy* (New York: Springer, 1982), 11–18.

13. Kübler-Ross, 140.

14. Larry A. Bugen, *Death and Dying: Theory/Research/Practice* (Dubuque, Iowa: Brown, 1979).

15. Kübler-Ross, 140–156.

16. Elisabeth Kübler-Ross, *Death: The Final Stage of Growth* (Englewood Cliffs, N.J.: Prentice-Hall, 1975), 117–167.

17. Hagglund, 242.

18. Kalish, 317.

19. Tappert, *Collection of Martin Luther,* "Treatise on Good Works," 110. C. S. Lewis, *The Problem of Pain* (New York: Macmillan, 1962).

20. Green, 1.

21. Sigmund Freud, *Mourning and Melancholia* (London: Hogarth, 1957), 243–258.

22. F. Lindemann, "Symptomatology and Management of Acute Grief," *American Journal of Psychiatry,* 101 (1944):141–149.

23. Worden, 11–18.

24. J. R. Calabrese et al., "Alterations in Immunocompetence During Stress, Bereavement, and Depression: Focus on Neuroendocrine Regulation," *American Journal of Psychiatry,* 144 (1987): 1123.

25. J. R. Calabrese et al., "Depression, Immunocompetence, and Prostaglandins of the E series," *Psychiatry Resident,* 17 (1986): 41–47. Z. Kronfol, "Leukocyte Regulation in Depression and Schizophrenia," *Psychiatry Resident,* 13 (1984):13–18. Z. Kronfol, "Depression, Cortisol Metabolism, and Lymphocytopenia," *Journal of Affective Disorders,* 9 (1985):169–173.

26. P. M. Mathews, "Enhancement of Natural Cytotoxicity by Beta Endorphin," *Journal of Immunology,* 130 (1983):1658–1662.

27. Kübler-Ross, *Death: The Final Stage of Growth,* 117.

## Chapter 2 Understanding Illness

1. Arthur J. Vander et al., *Human Physiology,* 2d ed. (New York: McGraw-Hill Book Company, 1975), 124.

2. Stanley L. Robbins, *Pathologic Basis of Disease* (Philadelphia: W. B. Saunders, 1974), 194–255.

3. Ibid., 55–103.

4. Ibid.

5. Paul Brand and Phillip Yancy, *Fearfully and Wonderfully Made* (Grand Rapids, Mich.: Zondervan, 1981), 37.

6. Gary R. Collins, *Christian Counseling, A Comprehensive Guide* (Waco, Tex.: Word, 1980), 401. Lawrence C. Kolb, *Modern Clinical Psychiatry* (Philadelphia: W. R. Saunders, 1977), 113–115.

7. Stephen A. Green, *Mind and Body, The Psychology of Physical Illness* (Washington, D.C.: American Psychiatric Press, 1985), 1.

8. Wolfgang K. Joklik, *Zinsser Microbiology,* 16th ed. (New York: Appleton-Century-Crofts, 1976), 2–3.

9. *American Family Physician,* Vol. 38, no. 2, 110.

10. R. E. Dubois et al., "Chronic Mononucleosis Syndrome," *Southern Medical Journal* 77 (November 1984):1356–1382.

11. J. L. Decker et al., "Rheumatoid Arthritis: Evolving Concepts of Pathogenesis and Treatment," *Annals of Internal Medicine* 101 (December 1984):810–824.

12. Marc C. Hochberg, "Osteoarthritis: Pathophysiology, Clinical Features, Management," *Hospital Practice* 19 (December 1984):41–53.

13. Peg Gray-Vickrey, "Evaluating Alzheimer's Patients," *Nursing 88*, 18 (December 1988):34–41.

14. Robert E. Rothenbern, *Health in the Later Years* (New York: New American Library, 1964), 188–194.

15. The chief causes of premature death include accidents, suicides, and murders related to alcohol. Lifestyle factors, such as smoking, cause 90 percent of lung diseases, including pneumonia, chronic obstructive lung disease, and lung cancer. Smoking also causes other cancers and contributes to hypertension, strokes, and heart disease. Diseases from alcoholism and drug abuse (such as cirrhosis, liver disease, withdrawal ailments, and overdosages) also kill many. If you add abortion to the statistics, over 95 percent of all premature deaths are due to preventable causes. For 1984–85 alone, an estimated 77 million years of potential life were lost. These statistics are taken from the *Mortality and Morbidity Weekly Report Supplement* (December 1986).

16. R. M. Rose, "Endocrine Responses to Stressful Psychological Events," *Psychiatric Clinics of North America* 3 (1980):251–276.

17. Hans Selye, *The Stress of Life* (New York: McGraw-Hill, 1956), 128–148.

18. Norman Cousins, *Anatomy of an Illness* (Toronto: Bantam Books, 1979), 39–40.

19. "Endorphins: A Role in Heart Disease?" *Science News* 130, 132.


## Chapter 3  Health Care and Illness

1. Lu Ann Aday, *Health Care in the U.S.* (Beverly Hills, Calif.: Sage Publications, 1980), 179–181.

2. *American Family Physician* 36 (July 1987):17.

3. E. G. Jaco, *Patients, Physicians and Illness* (New York: The Free Press, 1972), 222–233.

4. David Pendleton and John Hasler, eds., *Doctor-Patient Communication* (London: Academic Press, 1983), 90–104.

5. Ibid., 83.

6. Jaco, 220.

7. William Osler, *Aequanimitas* (New York: McGraw-Hill, 1906).

8. Quote attributed to Dr. William Henry Welch by Rene Dubos.

9. N. S. Hogan, *Humanizing Health Care* (Oradell, N.J.: Medical Economics Company, 1980).

10. S. G. Burger, *Living in a Nursing Home: A Complete Guide* (New York: The Seabury Press, 1976), 44–73.

11. Information and statistics from interview with administrator of the Pemberville/Portage Valley Nursing Home, January 1989.

12. David W. Aycock, *The Healing Art of Encouragement* (Wheaton, Ill.: Victor Books, 1987), 125–139.

13. Harriet Copperman, *Dying at Home* (New York: John Wiley and Sons, 1983), 83–96. R. Kopp, *When Someone You Love Is Dying: A Handbook for Counselors and Those Who Care* (Grand Rapids, Mich.: Zondervan, 1985).

14. C. A. Corr, *Hospice Care: Principles and Practice* (New York: Springer Publishing Co., 1983), 42–52. J. Abbout, *Hospice Resource Manual for Local Churches* (New York: Pilgrim Publishing, 1988). Martocchio et al., "Hospice: Compassionate Care and the Dying Experience," *Nursing Clinics of North America* 20 (2):269–280.

15. F. E. Moss, *Too Old, Too Sick, Too Bad* (Germantown, Md.: Aspen Systems, 1977), 73–102, 204–205.

## Chapter 4  Counseling and Illness

1. Edmond H. Babbit, *The Pastor's Pocket Manual for Hospital and Sickroom* (New York: Abingdon Press, 1948), 35. A. H. Becher, *The Compassionate Visitor: Resources for Ministering to People Who Are Ill* (Minneapolis, Minn.: Augsburg Publishing House, 1985).

2. J. Donald Bane, *Death and Ministry: Pastoral Care of the Dying and Bereaved* (New York: The Seabury Press, 1975), 61. J. M. Chaplin, *Together by Your Side: A Book for Comforting the Sick and Dying* (Notre Dame, Ind.: Ave Maria Publishing, 1979). M. Greenly, *Chronicle: The Human Side of AIDS* (New York: Irvington, 1986).

3. See *Mortality and Morbidity Weekly Report Supplement* (December 1986).

## Chapter 5  Counseling the Acutely and Critically Ill

1. Murray Grant, *Handbook of Community Health* (Philadelphia: Lea & Febiger, 1981), 57.

2. J. F. Fries and L. M. Crapo, *Vitality and Aging* (San Francisco: W. H. Freeman, 1981), 64.

3. V. A. Lambert and C. E. Lambert, *Psychosocial Care of the Physically Ill* (Englewood Cliffs, N.J.: Prentice-Hall, Inc., 1985), 8–20.

4. Therese A. Rando, *Grief, Dying and Death* (Champaign, Ill.: Research Press, 1984), 251–266.

5. V. Mor et al., "Secondary Morbidity Among the Recently Bereaved," *American Journal of Psychiatry* 143 (1986):158–163. M. Osterweis et al., *Bereavement: Reactions, Consequences, and Care* (Washington, D.C.: National Academy Press, 1984).

6. P. Clayton, "Mortality and Morbidity in the First Year of Widowhood," *Archives of General Psychiatry* 30 (1974):745–750. G. Engle, "Is Grief a Disease?" *Psychosomatic Medicine* 23 (1961):18–22.

7. J. J. Schiffers, *Family Medical Encyclopedia,* 2d ed. (New York: Pocket Books, 1983). American Medical Association Staff, *Family Medical Guide* (New York: Random House, 1982). *Family Medical Guide: The Illustrated Medical and Health Advisor* (New York: Morrow, 1983).

8. S. H. Johnson, *Long Term Care and the Law* (Owings Mills, Md.: National Health Publishing, 1983), 220–221. P. Goulden and B. Naitove, *Medical Science and the Law,* rev. ed. (New York: Facts on File Publications, 1984), 102–108. Laben and Powell, *Legal Issues and Guidelines: For Nurses Who Care for the Mentally Ill* (Thorofare, N.J.: SLACK, 1984), 15–17. Barton and Sanborn, *Law and the Mental Health Professions* (New York: International Universities Press, 1978), 216–218.

9. Paul Moody, *Decision Making: Proven Methods for Better Decisions* (New York: McGraw-Hill, 1983). R. N. Taylor, *Behavioral Decision Making* (Glenview, Ill.: Scott, Foresman and Co., 1984).

10. The American Cancer Society can be called toll free at (800) 227–2345. The Arthritis Foundation is located at 3400 Peachtree Road N.E., Atlanta, Georgia 30326. The Alzheimer's Association is located at 70 East Lake Street, Chicago, Illinois 60601. The organization's toll-free number is (800) 621–0379. Each of these three groups and the March of Dimes Birth Defects Foundation, the American Heart Association, the American Lung Association, and the American Diabetes Association also have local offices in many cities. Consult your local telephone directory for further information.

11. C. R. Lundahl, *A Collection of Near-Death Research Readings* (Chicago: Nelson-Hall Publishers, 1982), 117, 121. Michael B.

Sabom, *Recollections of Death: A Medical Investigation* (New York: Harper and Row, 1982), 22–23.

## Chapter 6  Counseling the Chronically Ill

1. Erdman B. Palmore, *Handbook of the Aged in the United States* (Westport, Conn.: Greenwood Press, 1984), 33.
2. G. E. Alan Dever, *Community Health Analysis, A Holistic Approach* (Germantown, Md.: Aspen Publications, 1980), 32.
3. Green, *Psychology of Physical Illness*, 12–13.
4. Ibid., 33–36.
5. Kolb, *Modern Clinical Psychiatry*, 124–125.
6. M. R. Castles and R. B. Murray, *Dying in an Institution: Nurse/Patient Perspectives* (New York: Appleton-Century-Crofts, 1979), 102.
7. Lambert and Lambert, *Psychosocial Care of the Physically Ill*, 18–19.
8. Twaddle, *Sickness Behavior*, 172–173. Palmore, *Handbook of the Aged*, 399–400. Moss and Halamandaris, *Too Old, Too Sick, Too Bad*, 112.
9. J. E. Meyer, *Death and Neurosis* (New York: International Universities Press, 1975), 67.
10. Copperman, *Dying at Home*, 46–47, 85, 91.
11. Adapted from *Depression*, Monograph 84, American Academy of Family Physicians, 1986, 26.
12. Adapted from *Anxiety*, Monograph 80, American Academy of Family Physicians, 1986, 19.
13. Adapted from *Geriatrics II*, Monograph 96, American Academy of Family Physicians, 1987, Table 7, 16.

## Chapter 7  Counseling the Psychiatrically Ill

1. Rodger K. Bufford, *Counseling and the Demonic*, Vol. 17, Resources for Christian Counseling (Dallas: Word, 1989).
2. V. B. Mountcastle et al., *Medical Physiology*, 14th ed. (St. Louis: C. V. Mosby, 1980), 46–81.
3. J. M. Kissane et al., *Anderson's Pathology*, 8th ed. (St. Louis: C. V. Mosby, 1985), 1820–1873.
4. Rene Spiegel, *Psychopharmacology: An Introduction* (New York: John Wiley and Sons, 1983), 94–97.

5. P. J. Dyck et al., *Peripheral Neuropathy* (Philadelphia: W. B. Saunders, 1984), 2162. John Gilroy et al., *Medical Neurology,* 3d ed. (New York: Macmillan, 1979), 304–309.

6. I. D. Anokhina et al., "Features of the Functioning of the Catecholamine and Adrenocortical Systems of Patients with Depression and Different Degrees of Emotional Tension," *Journal of Neuropathology and Psychiatry* 11 (1986):1703–1708. (Russian)

7. W. G. Joffe, "On the Concept of Pain, with Special Reference to Depression and Psychogenic Pain," *Journal of Psychosomatic Research* 11 (1967):69–75.

8. Adapted from Gregg R. Albers *Psychopharmacology,* Liberty School of Life Long Learning Worktext, 1987.

9. Raymond E. Vath, M.D., *Counseling Those with Eating Disorders,* Vol. 4 in Resources for Christian Counseling (Waco, Tex.: Word, 1986).

10. *Diagnostic and Statistical Manual of Mental Disorders, III,* American Psychiatric Association, 1980, 124.

11. *Geriatrics II,* Monograph 96, American Academy of Family Practice, 1987, 14.

12. Kolb, *Modern Clinical Psychiatry,* 251.

13. L. A. Amaducci et al., "Origin of the Distinction between Alzheimer's Disease and Senile Dementia: How History Can Clarify Nosology," *Neurology* 36, no. 11 (1986):1497–1499.

14. These groups exist worldwide. In the United States, write the Alzheimer's Association, 70 E. Lake St., Chicago, IL 60601; or call (800) 621–0379.

## Chapter 8 Counseling the Terminally Ill

1. Kalish, *Death, Grief and Caring Relationships.* Weizman and Kamm, *About Mourning.* Martocchio, *Hospice: Compassionate Care and the Dying Experience.* Paul Tournier, *Creative Suffering* (San Francisco: Harper and Row, 1983).

2. Worden, *Grief Counseling and Grief Therapy,* 32.

3. Parkes, *Bereavement.*

4. Bugen, *Death and Dying: Theory/Research/Practice,* 11–15. Worden, 58–63.

5. Kübler-Ross, *Death: The Final Stage of Growth,* 100.

6. Kalish, *Death, Grief, and Caring Relationships,* 184–185.

7. Worden, 53–58.

8. Rando, *Grief, Dying, and Death,* 44–48.

9. Ibid., 49–53.

10. Worden, 66–73.

11. Dorian et al., "Immune Mechanisms in Acute Psychological Stress," *Psychosomatic Medicine* 43 (1981):84.

12. Sabom, *Recollections of Death.*


## Chapter 9 Special Medical Situations

1. Beth Spring and Ed Larson, *Euthanasia: Spiritual, Medical and Legal Issues in Terminal Health Care* (Portland, Ore.: Multnomah Press, 1988), 21–41, 197–199.

2. This design for medical care guidance to family and physician appears to be original with the author. As suggested, it has no legal authority and could be used in combination with a living will or with a durable power of attorney. Just as medical information from a text is insufficient to treat a medical problem, so is legal information. This is not to be construed as legal advice. Please discuss these issues with your lawyer and recognize that laws may vary from state to state.

3. Franklin E. Payne, Jr., *Biblical Medical Ethics: The Christian and the Practice of Medicine* (Milford, Mich.: Mott Media, 1985), 184. See also Rev. 21:27.

4. Howard Brody, *Ethical Decisions in Medicine,* 2d ed. (Boston: Little, Brown & Co., 1981), 73–104.

5. This is a decision-making worksheet and should not be used as a point-scoring system or other device to decide when a person should be withdrawn from extraordinary care. It is designed only to help the family ask pertinent questions and to put them in an order that brings spiritual sense to the issue.

6. James Bopp, Jr., "Ethics of Abortion," *Human Life and Health Care Ethics* (Frederick, Md.: University Publications, 1985), 82–104.

7. This statistic is derived from averaging statistics published by the U.S. government and pro-life groups.

8. Payne, *Biblical Medical Ethics,* 150–151.

9. Everett L. Worthington, Jr., *Counseling for Unplanned Pregnancy and Infertility,* Vol. 10 in Resources for Christian Counseling (Waco, Tex.: Word, 1987).

10. Marshall B. Kapp, "Responses to the Living Will Furor: Directives for Maximum Care," *American Journal of Medicine* 72 (1982):856–857.

11. Spring and Larson, *Euthanasia,* 124.

12. Gerald L. Klerman, *Suicide and Depression Among Adolescents and Young Adults* (Washington, D.C.: American Psychiatric Press, 1986).

13. C. L. Hatton and S. Valente, *Suicide: Assessment and Intervention*, 2d ed. (Norwalk, Conn.: Appleton-Century-Crofts, 1984), 42–43. L. M. Gernsbacher, *The Suicide Syndrome* (New York: Human Sciences Press, 1985), 174–183.

## Chapter 10 Spiritual Fruit from Illness

1. M. E. Marty and K. L. Vaux, *Health/Medicine and the Faith Traditions: An Inquiry into Religion and Medicine* (Philadelphia: Fortress Press, 1982), 93–137.

2. Ibid., 274.

3. Ibid.

4. There is little documentation in the literature for some of the innovative health ministries contained in this chapter. Most have been personally observed by the author in various churches or ministries.

5. Collins, *Christian Counseling*, 14.

6. Many physicians still desire to serve irrespective of their present spiritual persuasion. Offering various ministry options, or offering to refer patients, is an excellent way to build a relationship that will lead to opportunities for sharing Christ.

7. A resource for church authority over a medical practice is Bill Gothard's Institute in Basic Youth Conflicts, Box 1, Oak Brook, IL 60521.

8. A working model of this situation is Liberty University Health Services, Box 20000, Lynchburg, VA 24506.

9. A working model of this situation is either Wheaton (Ill.) Medical Clinic, or the Kalamazoo (Mich.) Missionary Clinic. Also contact Liberty University Health Services; Christian Medical and Dental Society, Box 830689, Richardson, TX 75083-0689; or World Medical Mission, Box 3000, Boone, NC 28076.

10. A working model of this situation is the "Family Center," a ministry of Thomas Road Baptist Church, Lynchburg, Virginia.

11. A resource for ministry to the infirm elderly is the "Senior Saints Ministry," part of Thomas Road Baptist Church, 701 Thomas Road, Lynchburg, VA 24502.

12. A resource for the ministry to battered wives is the YWCA program. Another is Batterers Anonymous, Box 29, Redlands, CA 92373.

13. Examples are the LIFEAID Hotline, and Liberty Godparent Home Hotline, part of Thomas Road Baptist Church, Lynchburg, VA. Call (800) 543–3243 for further information.

14. A resource for further information or information packets is the Liberty Godparent Home and Network, Lynchburg, Va., (800) 543–3243.

15. A resource is Exodus International, P.O. Box 2121, San Rafael, CA 94912.

16. Liberty Health Service maintains a listing of potential speakers. Write Box 20000, Lynchburg, VA 24506 or call (804) 582–2514 for more information.

17. A resource for this type of ministry is Campus Crusade, Executive Ministries, 20 E. 73rd St., New York, NY 10021, (212) 517–4211.

# INDEX

## Gregg R. Albers, M.D., F.A.A.F.P.

Gregg R. Albers is a practicing family physician in Lynchburg, Virginia. He serves as director of Health Services at Liberty University and teaches at Liberty University and at the School of Life Long Learning and the Liberty Home Bible Institute. Dr. Albers is a member of the Christian Medical Society and the American Academy of Family Practice. In addition to a number of articles in specialty and Christian magazines, he has authored *Plague in Our Midst: Sexuality, AIDS, and the Christian Family.* He also produces and distributes a one-minute daily broadcast entitled "Health Journal," heard nationally on USA Radio network, Liberty Broadcasting Network, and Moody Radio Network.

Dr. Albers received his B.A. from Miami University, his M.D. from the Medical College of Ohio, and his Family Practice residency from Mercy Hospital, Toledo, Ohio. He and his wife Andrea are members of Thomas Road Baptist Church in Lynchburg, Virginia; they have two daughters, Bethany and Rachel, and two sons, Wesley and Andrew.